JOE BLAC

C000047556

A CLOW

Second Edition, Revised and Expanded

CLIPPER STUDIES IN THE THEATRE
ISSN 0748-237X * Number Six

by

Charles H. Day

Edited by William L. Slout

**The Borgo Press
An Imprint of Wildside Press**

MMVII

Copyright © 1993, 2007 by William L. Slout

Library of Congress Cataloging in Publication Data:

Blackburn, Joe, d. 1842.
    Joe Blackburn's A clown's log / by Charles H. Day ; edited by
William L. Slout. – 2nd ed., rev. and expanded.
    p. cm. — (Clipper studies in the theatre, ISSN 0748-237X ; no. 6)
    Rev. ed. of: An annotated narrative of Joe Blackburn's A clown's
log, 1993. A clown's log was first published in serial form in the New
York clipper in 1880.
    Includes bibliographical references and index.
    ISBN 0-8095-0307-7. — ISBN 0-8095-1307-2 (pbk.)
    1. Blackburn, Joe, d. 1842—Diaries. 2. Clowns—United States—
Diaries. 3. Clowns—United States—Biography. 4. Clowns—United
States—History—19th century. 5. Circus—England—History—19th
century. I. Day, Charles H., 1842-1907. II. Slout, William L. (William
Lawrence) III. Title. IV. Series.
GV1811.B54A3 2007   97-36044
791.3'3'092 [B]—dc21   CIP

SECOND EDITION

TABLE OF CONTENTS

Preface

Joseph Blackburn, in company with Levi J. North, visited the British Isles in 1838. An account of this trip appeared in serialized issues of the New York *Clipper*.[1] The entries were submitted by Charles H. Day with the elaborate heading: "A Clown's Log, Extracts from the Diary of the Late Joseph Blackburn, Chronicling Incidents of Travel with Circuses in the United States and England Forty Years Ago, with His Opinions of and Allusions to Professionals of the Period." According to Day, the excerpts were taken from eleven "passbooks" written in pencil and in a hand that was difficult to decipher. They were given to North by Blackburn's uncle, Thomas Atkinson of Lexington, KY.

I assume that Day was allowed access to the material by North. Day had interviewed him for an articled about his career which was later carried in the New York *Clipper* of March, 1880, only a month following Day's series of "A Clown's Log." It may be that the log was obtained or copied at that meeting. In Day's words:

> Some years since, I wrote for the New York *Clipper* an extended account of [North's] most brilliant career at home and abroad. It was with much difficulty and only after the most persistent persuasion that I succeeded in securing from his lips the necessary data.... Howard or Fontaine of the *Herald* afterward tried to get from the veteran's lips the events of his professional career; and although his warm friend, William J. Florence, interceded, the ex-equestrian's consent could not be obtained.[2]

In presenting "A Clown's Log," Day assured his readers that it followed "the identical language of the author, without embellishment or addition by the editor," and that the omissions from the original text were items "not of general interest to the readers of an amusement journal." It is unfortunate that Blackburn's manuscript has not been located at this writing. The omitted passages might indeed be of interest to us and add to our understanding of this intriguing clown. I was informed by Fred D. Pfening III that some years ago Arthur H. Saxon attempted to find the diaries by seeking out the heirs of Charles Day; but, sadly, the effort was fruitless.

The brackets within the memoirs contain Day's insertions. Some alteration of punctuation has been done in editing. Blackburn's and Day's text is italicized to avoid confusion with the Slout annotations.

Blackburn's diary is a unique contribution to the history of the early American circus; but it is more than that, more than a useful historical record. It is a brief revelation of Joe Blackburn as a living, breathing person, one who could be elated, disdainful, surprised, convivial, bemused, and all the other emotional and intellectual responses that are normal to one's living moments as he encounters the changing elements around him. I was intrigued by this human sampling of early nineteenth century vitality. I wanted to join with Joe and Levi and accompany them on their adventurous trip to England. So I did join them in the only way I could. I followed their travels, got to know the people they met along the way, and envisioned the places they visited. And I enjoyed my literary vacation, every mile of it. Now, I invite you, the reader of this travelogue, to join Joe and Levi and me as we hit the road that takes us from New Orleans to England and back home again. Here's to a pleasant journey!

William L. Slout

Prologue

Charles H. Day (1842?-1907) was one of the leading press agents and bill writers of his era. Early in his career as agent, he was connected with negro minstrelsy, troupes headed by such luminaries as William Arlington, W. W. Newcomb, Sam Sharpley, and W. S. Cleveland. He joined actress Laura Keene's dramatic company at the Chestnut Street Theatre, Philadelphia, in 1869 and remained in her employ for a tour of the West. In 1871, while with Newcomb & Arlington's Minstrels, Twenty-Eighth Street near Broadway, N.Y.C., he became New York theatrical correspondent for John Stetson's *Sporting Times* and an occasional contributor to the Sunday New York *Mercury*.[3] That year he placed an advertisement in the New York *Clipper*:[4]

Charles Day
To Managers of First-Class
Circuses and Menageries
CHARLES H. DAY
New York Correspondent of the *Sporting Times*, Author of "Humors of Show Life," published in the *New York Mercury*; also "Alice Drayton," "Jersey Blues," "Actress and Minstrel," "Up Hill" and numerous other novelettes, can be secured as
WRITER
for the Tenting Season of '72 and '73 by any Responsible Management. Five years' experience as an Advertiser. Two years Agent and Business Manager with Miss Laura Keene. Address care St. Charles Hotel, 648 Broadway, N.Y.

From this effort, Day was taken on as director of publications by John H. Murray, with whose circus he remained for three years. Circus life seems to have fit his style; for, upon leaving the Murray show, he was employed as agent for L. B. Lent's Circus (1876), Den W. Stone's (1878), W. C. Coup's Equescurriculum (1878), Adam Forepaugh's (1879-81, 1887), Cooper, Jackson & Co. (1882), Barnum & London (1884), Sells Bros.' (1886), etc.

Day, the press agent, was considered by his colleagues to be "a man of energy and resource," a gentleman of the old school and a congenial, convivial companion. He was noted for his originality of composition, his ability to put on paper that "which oft was thought but ne'er so well expressed." His couriers were described as "surpassing in range of thought and vividness any published by circuses at that time." One of his catch lines for John H. Murray, during the season of 1874, was "Refined gold needs no gilding." In writing opposition bills, he straightforwardly described the shortcomings of rival shows in a frank and convincing manner. While with W. C. Coup, his tactic, relating to the VanAmburgh show that had ventured into Coup's territory, consisted of thousands of flyers, decorated with large, red stripes through the center, which read: "VanAmburgh Show Dissected! Postmortem of a Galvanized Corpse!" With Forepaugh in 1875, he edited a sixteen-page newspaper handout, *The Adam Forepaugh Illustrated Feature Journal*, in which he included household hints, recipes, remedies for common ailments, and a children's department. He is given credit for the idea of Forepaugh's $10,000 Beauty Contest and the prearranged selection of Louise Montague as the winner, first brought out for the season of 1881, and used as a feature of the street pageant, "Lalla

Rookh's Departure from Delhi," with Miss Montague paraded atop the famous elephant in all her splendor.[5]

As a free lance writer, Day published more than one hundred pieces. Beginning in the 1870s and for the next thirty-five years, he was an occasional contributor to such circus and theatrical publications as the *Clipper, Billboard, Sporting and Theatrical Journal,* and *New York Dramatic Mirror.* A series of stories for the *Home Magazine* began in 1899 with "Tales of the Circus Man." In 1900, "VanAmburgh, Elephant Performer and Lion Trainer" was serialized in *Golden Hours* and then turned into book form.

Following his retirement, at the age of fifty-nine, Day married the twenty-three year old Gertrude H. Garvey of New York City on November 29, 1901. He died in New Haven, CT, six years later, October 3, 1907, presumably unprovoked by the spousal age differential, the cause being erysipelas.

Joe Blackburn, the clown and author of these memoirs, was said to have been born in Baltimore by two different sources, T. Allston Brown and Charles Durang. However, the diary confirms his birthplace as England. Still, as Day mentions in his introduction to these extracts, "he was in sentiment and politics a Yankee and a Republican." When it was once suggested by an English performer that Blackburn's feet would benefit from a bath, the clown displayed them with pride as he replied, "That's the land of liberty."

Durang has suggested that Blackburn was trained for the Catholic priesthood, which may or may not be accurate; but he appears to have had the benefit of some formal schooling. Multi-talented, he was one of a few early circus people to keep a log of his activities, and his letters occasional from England were published in several of the American newspapers. He was the composer of at least one song, "Sich a Gettin' Up Stairs," which he probably used in the ring; but the piece was also performed on the New York stage by a variety of comedians around the time of our narrative.[6]

It is likely that Blackburn, a clown who juggled on horseback, was a performer of some ability. Durang referred to him as "the most celebrated among racy and droll clowns, combining uncommon humor and visual activity," an asset which led to his being dubbed the "American Grimaldi." T. Allston Brown nominated him *the* clown of the American arena. "He was a man of most extraordinary ability," Brown wrote. "He possessed a good education and figured as a poet of no ordinary pretensions."[7] And because of his gentle good humor and affability, he was often referred to as "Gentleman Joe." During his career, he was connected with various circus organizations from as early as 1825 until his final engagement in 1841.

It is apparent from his writing that, out of the ring, Blackburn was a man of varied interests. He was a frequent theatergoer and a willing judge of actors' successes or failures. He was an habitual visitor of places where beverages were dispensed and where late night conversation was the featured attraction. His observations throughout his travels suggest an interest in things around him. He apparently loved sports and mingling with men of the sporting world. And, not least, politics and nationalism were elements of concern and often influenced his assessment of people and events.

Blackburn's journey begins in New Orleans in 1838, where he and the great rider and tumbler, Levi J. North, were performing with the circus of Noell E. Waring. The city of New Orleans was composed of nearly 100,000 people. Its population encompassed an international spectrum—French, Spanish, Scandinavian, Dutch, English, and, because of the potato famine of the 1830s, Irish by the shiploads. Add to this, Americans from all parts of the continent and the homogeneity is complete. The city was like one huge vacuum cleaner, sucking in humanity from both sea and river. But it was a city of contradiction. On one hand, it was called a pest hole. A major port in a hot, semi-topical *milieu*, it was susceptible to the pestilence brought in through maritime activity from all parts of the world. Plagues of cholera, small pox, and yellow fever were dreaded catastrophes which recurred nearly every decade. Still, it was a "good time town." Someone once wrote, "Thank God the French got here first. Can you imagine what New Orleans might have been had the Pilgrims gotten off at Pilottown instead of Plymouth?"[8] Art was abundant, and music filled the air, and sporting events electrified the multi-ethnic populous. Dog fights were traditional, and horse racing. In 1837, the Eclipse race course introduced the first all-thoroughbred competitions. Prize fighting had its audience. The city's first official encounter occurred in 1836 between "Deaf" Burke and Sam O'Rourke, a popular contest of Englishman vs. Irishman. And then there was the traditional Mardi Gras. In our year of 1838, the festival was bigger and better than ever. *La Creole* reported that "the whole town doubled up with laughter."[9] Dramatic performances were also capturing a sizable share of public interest. The new St. Charles, the most magnificent theatre in the South, under the management of James Caldwell, first opened its doors for the 1835-36 season. The rival American Theatre, under the guidance of Richard Russell, offered a varied and somewhat lower order of entertainment. Yes, New Orleans was a seamy, steamy, dreadful, boisterous, joyous city when Blackburn and North performed there in 1838.

Nor were circus performances new to the residents of New Orleans. As early as 1821, Victor Pepin brought his troupe there and performed in the converted St. Philip Street Theatre. More recently, it was Brown territory: first J. Purdy in 1833 and 1834, and then Oscar with Brown & Co. in 1836. But it appears that this was a new stand for Waring's winter circus when the company made a jump there from Natchez and remained from December 23, 1837, through January 22, 1838.[10]

Manager Noell E. Waring (d. 1854) was one of the earliest exhibitors of traveling menageries in the United States. He was associated with the firm of Raymond & Waring for several years and remained active in the circus business almost to the time of his death in this very city.

Levi J. North (1814-1885) was born in Newtown township, Long Island. In 1826, he apprenticed to Isaac Quick of Quick & Mead's circus and toured the South. In the fall of 1828, the management built the Washington Circus on the old York Road, Northern Liberties, Philadelphia, where they produced a variety of equestrian dramas. The company traveled to towns in Pennsylvania with the coming of spring; but, by summer's end and time for the 1829 winter season to begin, the circus troupe returned to the comfort of Philadelphia. North's apprenticeship was terminated at this point.[11] He then engaged with Welch & Handy for exhibitions in Cuba, the West Indies, and South America, at the sum of thirty dollars a month. On returning to the United States, he joined J. Purdy Brown's company in 1832, and remained until Brown's death four years later; after which, Oscar Brown took over the circus for a while and then combined it with Fogg & Stickney. Both Blackburn and North were connected with the company during the 1836 season. North was with it again in 1837.[12] The following winter, he joined a group of performers who were conducting a show on the commonwealth plan in Louisville, KY. But, when the clouds of unfriendly winter faded and kindly spring appeared, North packed his gear and traveled down river to New Orleans and connected with Waring's troupe.[13] At this point, Blackburn and North met up again and decided to take a professional trip to England.[14]

The two were accompanied on their transAtlantic journey by friends Barkham Cony and Master William Blanchard. Cony, often called the "dog star," was famous for his roles in canine melodramas, which featured his trained dogs, Hector and Bruin. An active and muscular man, he was quite handy as a boxer, yet charitable and good-hearted. He came into prominence in London at the Cobourg Theatre in 1828. This was followed with profitable engagements in the established houses of both England and America. He first introduced his wares to an American audience at the Bowery Theatre, N.Y.C., on May 8, 1836, in "The Forest of Bondy." Durang called him "a very clever pantomimist of the minor theatre school."[15] While visiting the United States for the third time, he died in Chicago, January 1, 1858, at the age of 56.

Young Blanchard assisted Cony in the dramatic pieces, playing second to him. He was described by Ireland as an agile and dexterous performer.[16] In growing into manhood, he became large and stout, unsuitable for the line of roles he was called upon to perform. Yet he remained in the dog acting business until Cony's death, after which he returned to England where he engaged in performing and producing pantomimes.

"Dog stars" were a popular phenomenon in the first part of the century. They traveled in pairs, one to enact the virtuous character, always accompanied by his faithful canine, and the other the unsavory or villainous role. "The seize," as it was called, occurred at the climax of the melodrama when, at a given signal, the bowser sprang at the malefactor's throat and held on until the deserving victim relented or expired. Around this time, an English "dog star," one Jack Matthews, laid claim to being the only "Dog Hamlet." The scurrilous half-hour version of Shakespeare's masterpiece was performed at English booth shows and fairs. In it, the melancholy Dane was followed around the stage by a large black dog, who would "bay the moon" at the sight of the Ghost and throttle the King in the final scene.[17]

Early in March, Blackburn and party left New Orleans by boat for a stopover in Mobile, possibly for a Cony and Blanchard commitment at the St. Emanuel Street Theatre, managed by Noah Ludlow. Travel from New Orleans to the port city of Mobile took

them along the shoreline of the Gulf into Mobile Bay,
a distance of nearly two hundred miles. The bay was
formed by the convergence of the Alabama and Tom-
bigbee Rivers. Two major sand bars between the port
of the city and the lower bay necessitated the cargo of
ocean-going vessels to be unloaded onto flat-bottom
boats and towed to the Mobile docks; and the same
encumbrance inconvenienced passenger travel as
well. In spite of this, Mobile was undergoing a decade of boom years. King Cotton had begun its reign.
The removal of the Indians to a region west of the
Mississippi opened up rich land where acreage was
cleared and cotton was planted to become the great
staple crop of the area. Along the rivers running to
the Gulf there were hundreds of private landings
where river boats could take on cargo and carry it to
the port of Mobile. Agents from throughout the world
opened offices from which to buy the harvest and ship
it back to their home countries. Hundreds of boats
became crowded along Mobile's river front, piled
high with cotton bales for transport overseas. This
new prosperity swelled Mobile's population during
the 1830s from about 3,000 to nearly 35,000. In our
year of 1838, it was a bustling, barge-toting, bale-
lifting, enterprising little metropolis, where the theatre was about the only regular amusement Mobilians
had. In reality, Mobile and New Orleans were the
only cities in the Deep South to have a continuing
winter season of theatrical entertainment.[18]

       J. Purdy Brown erected Mobile's St. Emanuel
Street Theatre in 1833 to house his theatrical and
equestrian companies, and opened it in the spring of
the following year. He engaged three stars as his initial attractions, only to find that after the accounts

were settled there was nothing left for himself. "Poor fellow!" Noah Ludlow wrote, "that or a late crab supper killed him, and I rented his building the ensuing fall for dramatic purposes alone, and retained it for five years."[19]

When Blackburn and North arrived in Mobile, Yankee Hill was playing a starring engagement for Ludlow. He had appeared in New Orleans at the American Theatre six weeks earlier, performing his roles in "The Forest Rose" and "The Yankee Pedlar." George Handel Hill (d. 1849), a native New Englander, is looked upon as the foremost delineator of the "Yankee" character on the American stage. At this time, at a mere twenty-eight years of age, he was near the peak of his career. He had experienced a stunning success in England only the year before. Even so, Blackburn's anticipated trip abroad interested Hill and he agreed to join the party for the Atlantic crossing.[20]

So decided, Blackburn and North left Mobile for the East Coast. The first leg of their trip took them up the twisting and turning Alabama River to Montgomery. From there they rode the stage over the Fall Line hills and across the full width of Georgia to Augusta, situated adjacent to the South Carolina border.

Stage travel in America was not pleasant. The roads were rough and rutted in the best of weather. Heavy rain and flood water made them nearly unusable at certain times of the year. The coaches, built for durability under such conditions, jarred and jolted the riders about in a manner unimaginable to our generation. The lengthy journey from Montgomery to Augusta must have been unpleasant indeed.

Once they arrived in Augusta, Blackburn and North presumably continued by train on the South Carolina Railroad, which had been completed in 1833. Starting from Hamburg, just opposite Augusta on the Savannah River, the tracks moved southeastward into the coastal plain and on to the port city of Charleston. At a distance of 136 miles, it was the longest passenger steam railroad in the world at that period of development.

One can only estimate how many days had passed from the time Blackburn and North left New Orleans. The circus ended its stand there on January 22. Yankee Hill finished his engagement on February 12 and must have gone directly to Mobile. Blackburn and North's whereabouts between those dates are unaccounted; but, as the diary begins, after a period of some seven weeks since leaving the circus, Blackburn and North arrived at Charleston in March of 1838.

Blackburn in America

Charleston, the chief city of South Carolina, was originally located on a narrow peninsula where, it was once said, the Ashley and Cooper Rivers "unite to form the Atlantic Ocean." As part of what was called the Low Country, the city was situated on a site so low that its sewers were below sea level, which prompted one observer to remark that the odors that filled the summer air were a mixture of "heavy salt, pluff mud, oleanders, and drains."[21] The population was composed of English, French, Scotch, German, and Irish. Picturesque narrow streets were lined with stately homes of 18th century architecture, tall, slate-roofed, and built flush to the street. At the time of our travelers, the city boasted of the world's first department store, an extraordinarily large building erected on the corner of King and Market Streets. The Planters Hotel, famous for its food and Planters Punch, was the social center of a city, where industries of rice, cotton, and shipping had created a healthy level of prosperity.

Monday, 19. [After speaking of the Tower of Babel scene at the depot, and the wranglings of the baggage men, omnibus drivers and hotel runners, it says:] Drove for Shelton's. Brushed and took a drink, which they did not charge for. That made me have a good opinion of the house from the start. After supper, visited the new theatre, under the management of Abbott---one of the most beautiful theatres I was ever in.

The new theatre in Charleston had just opened on December 15, 1837; at which time, the management was applauded by the *Spirit of the Times* for promoting respectability and quiet within the establishment through abolishing the sale of "ardent spirits." Obviously, this move was made at considerable sacrifice, for such sales amounted to several thousand dollars a season. The managers were William Abbott and W. H. Latham, who were also lessees of the Washington, Buffalo and Montreal theatres.

Abbott (1760-1843) was born in Chelsea, England. At age seventeen he made his debut at the Bath theatre as *Alonzo* in "Pizarro," which led to his being engaged at that place for four years. There followed London appearances at the Haymarket and Covent Garden, and then on to America. As to his acting, Durang wrote that "in parts denominated walking gentlemen, he displayed that acute sense of propriety of emphasis that at times renders the lackadaisical dialogue of modern comedy truly impressive."[22] Although cumbersome in form, the assessment is made by a man who was for many years a shrewd observer of theatrical endeavor. Abbott was felled senseless by a stroke on May 31, 1843, while performing on the Park stage in Shield's "The Apostate," and lingered in a weakened state for a week before he passed on. It is pleasing to report that he was remembered by his friends as a person of cheerful disposition, of polished manners, and a conversationalist of wit and humor.[23]

Latham first appeared on the American stage at the New York's Park Theatre in September of 1835. Ireland described him as "an excellent comic actor, and a buffo singer of great merit."[24] He died a year after Abbott.

> *Booth played Sir Giles Overreach, Flynn---. Booth had just recovered from one of his crazy fits, in which he had broken an iron fire dog over Flynn's head. A hard head that Flynn has got.*

The character of *Overreach*, from Philip Massinger's comedy "New Way to Pay Old Debts," was a standard in Booth's repertory. His co-star, Thomas Flynn (1798-1849), was another of the many English importations during the early part of the century, and whom Noah Ludlow observed as "a man that effected more extraordinary things in acting and management than any one I ever heard of, with so limited amount of money and talents."[25]

Junius Brutus Booth (1796-1852) and Thomas Flynn were good friends. Nevertheless, while sharing a room with Booth at the Planter's Hotel in Charleston, Flynn was awakened one night, some time after 1:00 a.m., by a blow to his head. He sprang up to discover Booth standing above him with a raised andiron, ready to swing again. Flynn's attempt to avoid a second blow was unsuccessful; the cast-iron fire dog was broken as it landed on his forehead, just above the eye. Flynn's calls brought assistance and Booth was restrained until his temporary derangement went away.[26] But Flynn must have got in a few licks as well. George Stone recalls that Booth's nose was broken in the fray, which caused a marked nasal sound in his speech ever after. It was generally known, as Stone described it, that liquor would "frequently produce upon him a state of frenzy that was sometimes

terrible, and when these fits were on, he would as
soon attack friend as foe." Stone's version of this
confrontation is somewhat different. He has Booth
returning from the theatre—perhaps after having
stopped for refreshment along the way—still dressed
in the stage costume of *Iago*. As he menacingly ap-
proached Flynn, he recited: "Nothing can or shall
content my soul 'till I am even with him, wife for
wife; or failing so, yet that I have put the Moor at
least into a jealousy so strong, that judgment cannot
cure."

It was at this point that Flynn, in self-defense,
hit Booth on the nose, breaking it, with a "fire poker
or tongs." Poor Flynn idolized Booth. Ever after,
whenever the subject of the incident was brought up
in Flynn's presence, he would burst into tears.[27]

*[In another place, he speaks of Booth's "Rich-
ard III" disparagingly: "Left after the third act," but
adds that Booth played "Othello" beautifully.]*
Nov. 22.[28] *[He writes:] Attended the theatre.
Saw Booth's "Lear"---the best acting I ever saw.
[During his stay in Charleston, he mentions meeting
Booth on the street, and says:] Booth looks debili-
tated. [Of Washington, what he saw there, and whom
he met, he writes:] At the circus saw Charley Barton,
Henry Madigan, John Robinson, Frank Willmot and
Alex Rockwell.*

We don't know when Blackburn and North arrived in Washington; however, Stuart Thayer has
placed the circus there during the time of March 26-
28.[29] The men must have taken a boat from Charles-

ton, north past Cape Hatteras and Norfolk, into Chesapeake Bay and up the Potomac River.

In Washington, North and Blackburn connected with Charles H. Bacon's Circus. Bacon was an eight year old apprentice rider during the initial season at the Lafayette Amphitheatre, N.Y.C., in 1825. Subsequently, he was connected with Price & Simpson, Aaron Turner, William Blanchard, Fogg & Stickney, William Harrington, James W. Bancker, Nathan A. Howes, and finally, in 1837, he became the proprietor of his own company. I cannot identify Charley Barton, but through his association with the others one might assume he was a circus man. There was a general performer named Barton in H. P. Madigan's company of 1856. Or could the name in Blackburn's original text have been Charles Bacon, the circus proprietor? Alex Rockwell, equestrian and clown of note, is probably the Master Alexander whom Thayer has listed with the troupe at the time.[30] Frank Wilmot was a scenic and two-horse rider. Henry Madigan and John Robinson were equestrians who later became prominent circus proprietors.

Henry P. Madigan (1815-1862) was a native of Albany, NY, who became the patriarch of a talented Madigan circus family, consisting of Henry P., his wife Marie, and their children Emma, Ella, Rose, Eggie, James, and Charles. During a career which began as early as 1826 with the Albany Circus, he was considered a daring rider. He went into management for the first time in 1850 as Stone & Madigan's Great Southwestern Circus. In his unpublished "manuscript," agent John Dingess said of him: "Whether as ringmaster, equestrian, gymnast, vaulter, pantomimist or brilliant invention, Henry P. Madigan had no superior.... His accomplishment made up an entire encyclopedia of the sports of the circle.... His disposition was one of the most amiable character and his habits excellent."

John F. Robinson (1807?-1888), often called "Old John" to distinguish him from his son, became founder and long-time owner of John Robinson' Circus and one of the great individuals in circus history. He was a physical giant of a man, with incredible strength in his prime. It was said he had been known to kill an unruly horse with one blow of his fist. Although a person of charitable inclinations, he was profane and quick tempered, described as being impulsive, strong-headed, blunt, laconic, and outspoken. He died leaving an estate valued at over $1,000,000.

Tuesday, 27. After breakfast, saw Bacon and made an engagement for Levi North and myself for four weeks, commencing tomorrow night with "The Seven Living Pictures." Took a walk to the capital, Jim Wills, Alex Rockwell and myself. Had a pleasant time of it. Visited the House of Representatives, the Senate, and, last but not least, the refectory, where we took a glass of wine each. They did not sell anything stronger. I suppose by that that the heads of the nation must be quite temperate.

Blackburn must have known James Wills for some time. In 1835, for Radcliffe's benefit at the American Theatre, New Orleans, he performed *Richmond* to Wills' *Richard* in a scene from "Richard III." Shortly after Wills' Washington residency, on July 18, the actor appeared at the Walnut Street Theatre, Philadelphia. The following year in Natchez he cut his throat and died.

Went to the theatre [managed by Ward, of whom Blackburn writes: "is a perfect gentleman."] Mossop's benefit; played "The Battle of Algiers;" the last scene, panoramic view of the port, very beautiful and effective.

The National Theatre, Washington, DC, was just opened under Thomas Ward's management on January 1, 1838. Ward was an Englishman, born in Liverpool in 1799. He had been stage manager at the Walnut Street Theatre, Philadelphia, prior to his Washington proprietorship. "Let me assure you that it requires no common patience and perseverance to manage a theatre," wrote the *Spirit of the Times* correspondent regarding the opening of the season, "for the drama has two powerful rivals in politics and parties, and the actor who sees the house two-thirds filled may consider himself to have achieved a triumph." This item was prophetic. A short time later, the paper praised Ward for supporting the drama in Washington, but added, "Each week a new star rises by his perseverance, yet it is seldom that the theatre is crowded."[31] The Washington season closed on March 31, an indication of the languishing state of the drama in the nation's capital.

George Mossop (1814-1849), a Dublin born actor, was described by Ireland as "a light, trim-built young fellow, and ambitious of a distinction in music and Irish comedy which he never reached."[32] He was married to Mrs. Harry Knight for a while and later to

Mrs. Henry Hunt (Mrs. John Drew). Mossop died in Albany, N.Y.

Wednesday, 28. Played ringmaster to Levi's riding. He got along pretty well, having a strange horse. Vaulting bad---only about twenty. [While playing in Washington, he made a flying trip to Baltimore, and complains because "the Harrisburg bills, taken at the other end of the line, were refused at the Baltimore depot," and speaks of the cars being drawn by horses a mile from the depot.[33]

In writing of a week's performance at Fredericksburg, Virginia, the receipts are spoken of as "good"—from $150 to $100 a day—and the company leaving well pleased with the town, and the town well pleased with the company.]

Sunday, (April) 8. Drove twenty-two miles to Bowling Green in a heavy rain. One mile out of town a large wagon we had hired to take part of baggage upset over a bank---a beautiful mess of little boys, trunks, Dutch musicians and other et ceteras piled up together. Nobody hurt. Got wagon up and started. Rain began getting rather damp. Had to bear for eleven mile tavern ahead. Stopped, got liquor, bread and meat, and a good fire. Paid dollar for refreshments for six.

[The next day:] The sun has shown its face once more. Played at two o'clock in the after-noon and again at night. Took in about $150. People well pleased, and a majority well drunk. Only interruption during the night was a squid let off by John Robinson for a lark.[34]

[On the same page, without naming the town, he speaks of Levi doing forty-one somersaults.]

Bacon's circus was working its way from Washington to Richmond. The company was in Alexandria, March 29-31, a few miles down the Potomac. The jump to Fredericksburg for April 2-7 was about fifty miles. The stand in Bowling Green on April 9 was a twenty-five mile move. Thayer found no evidence of a booking between Bowling Green and Richmond.[35] The Richmond dates were April 13-21

Richmond is located nearly 100 miles southwest of Washington at the head of navigation on the James River, bordered by rolling hills to the north and south. A port of entry for Virginia, it was even then the capital, its edifice being constructed between 1785 and 1792. The Richmond, Fredericksburg and Potomac Railroad carried its first passengers in 1836. It was a community of iron works, cotton mills, and tobacco warehouses; yet, with a population of under 10,000, a resort of the gay and fashionable.

[Arrived in Richmond, he begins Log No. 2.] Went to the theatre. Mrs. Harry Knight's benefit, a shocking bad house---about $20. The acting as bad as the house.

13th. Played at night. Full house. Levi did thirty-eight somersaults, and Friday rode only tolerably. Horses too bad.

The tragic Richmond theatre fire of December 26, 1811, which resulted in a great loss of life, left the city with no will to rebuild for several years. In 1818 a list of subscribers, which included Chief Justice John Marshall, funded the erection of a structure on Seventh and Broad Streets. It was some time later, however, before the theatre came into full use. In 1835 the *Southern Literary Messenger* noted that the place was "only occasionally patronized when the appearance of some attractive star or celebrated performer is advertised."[36]

Mrs. Knight was the daughter of John Kent, a long-time member of the Park Theatre company. Durang thought her to be an excellent general actress in comedy, tragedy and operatic pieces. She supported a fine figure, an expressive face, and always dressed with care and good taste. She married Henry Knight, the son of English actor Edward Knight of the Drury Lane Theatre, London. Unlike his father, Harry's acting was confined to servant and rustic roles. He met with an accident while en route from Philadelphia to Baltimore in 1839. His train had stopped at some point and Knight had got off for refreshments; but before he could re-board, the train began to move. In his effort to get back onto it, he slipped and fell. One leg was run over by a car wheel. The leg was amputated in an attempt to save his life, but to no avail; he died in agony. The Knights were separated in 1837, but following the fatal accident, Mrs. Knight was at her ex-husband's side, administering to him through his final hours. She eventually married a Mr. DaCosta, a non-professional, and retired to Philadelphia.[37]

Monday, 15.[38] New arrivals to the company— Levi's old and particular friend, Ned Derious.

Saturday, 20. Theatre, with Booth as Sir Edward Mortimer and Mossop as Dr. O'Toole, to only about $50.37. The circus, on the contrary, played to a good house.[39]

Shortly after his arrival, Edwin Derious purchased a half interest in the circus, which became Bacon & Derious on April 22.[40] Derious (1808-1888) was born in Philadelphia. Throughout his career he was considered a proficiet vaulter, rider and tight rope performer. Prior to his appearance here, he had been connected with J. Purdy and Benjamin Brown and Joseph D. Palmer's circuses. He continued as a performer and manager with a variety of companies into the 1880s.

[The engagement of North and Blackburn having ended, he signifies it with:] Packed up one shirt in two sheets of paper, and am ready to start for Baltimore. [Evidently the clown indulged in humor out of the ring as well as in it. Under the same date, he continues:] Went to bed at twelve. Talked to Ned Derious until two o'clock about man-agement, he having bought half of Bacon's circus this day at $2,500.

[Blackburn left Richmond on board the Thomas Jefferson, and refers to the "celebrated horses, Atlanta and Boston, on board, returning from the Petersburg races."]

Even at this early time, wealthy planters were breeding racing stock and forming Jockey Clubs, and holding spring and fall races in Richmond and Petersburg. They "came to town in their coaches and four, in their phaetons, chariots and gigs," accompanied by their wives and daughters beribboned in the newest of spring and fall fashions. Race week was a veritable carnival—streets crowded with equipage, and shops, boarding houses, and taverns beset with frenetic activity. The social high point was the Race Ball, where the belle and beau met in all their finery to cavort through many a minuet and reel.

Richmond and Petersburg are closely situated, adjacent to the James River which spills into the mouth of Chesapeake Bay. Baltimore is located at the navigation head of the Patapsco River, twelve miles from the bay's northwest shore and about 170 miles from the Atlantic Ocean. Altogether, the trip from Richmond to Baltimore is nearly 300 miles by water. A land journey is less than half the distance. Assuming Blackburn's contract ended with the Richmond stand on April 21 and his arrival at Baltimore was no later than April 24, the first date listed in his diary, he made exceedingly good time.

Baltimore was one of the larger cities in the United States, with a citizenry of about 100,000. The city's accessibility to western produce made it competitive as a commercial port with New York and New Orleans. During this period, it was undergoing geographic expansion and population growth. Over 55,000 immigrants, mostly German and Irish, poured into the city during the 1830s. At the same time, Baltimore was experiencing an interval of deflation, which began in 1837 and would continue until 1843, making political controversies between Jacksonians and Whigs a lively contest.

[Arrived at Baltimore, at night he visited the theatre, plays being "Mons. Tonson" and "Kentuckian," Hackett as Nimrod Wildfire and Mons. Marbleau. Very good acting on his part, but bad house.][41]

Tuesday, 24. Took to the theatre. Plays, "Fazio" and "Jonathan in England;" Mrs. Sharpe as Bianca, excellent; Mr. Lewellan as Fazio, damned bad. Hackett in the last piece as Solomon Swap, almost as bad as Fazio---not nearly as good as Yankee Hill's.

"Fazio" was a tragedy by H. M. Milman, performed by Mrs. Sharpe for her opening night in Baltimore. She was the sister to James H. Hackett's wife. After migrating from England in 1824, she made her New York debut in November of that year at the Park Theatre, where she soon became a favorite. Ireland described her as "a tall, fine-looking woman, with dark eyes and hair, possessed of a good figure," and "altogether pleasing in her stage bearing."[42]

Lewellan, an Englishman and an actor of little note, made his American debut at the Chestnut Street Theatre, Philadelphia. Blackburn's observation of his performance is most likely accurate.

"Jonathan in England" was a comedy altered by Hackett from George Colman's "Who Wants a Guinea?" Hackett, of course, was an established star. He was a rival of Hill's in the portrayal of "Yankee" roles and nine years Hill's senior. The comedy character of *Solomon Swap* was in Hill's repertory as well. Blackburn may have been influenced by his friendship with Hill in condemning Hackett's performance, even though Hill was the superior "Yankee" actor.

Monday, 25.[43] Election for Representative to Congress; Jim Wills' vote challenged by a Greek. Born in the ward and living twenty-three years in it, he thought it best to get naturalized, and possibly he might vote then without being insulted. His vote was finally taken.

[Next day North arrived from Richmond, and he showed him about the town. Again quoting the diary:] Went to the theatre. Took the whole family. Hackett's benefit, good house. Plays, "Mons. Mallet" and "Perfection,"[44] in which Mrs. Sharpe appeared. And "Henry IV;" Hackett as Sir John only tolerable. [The next day he sailed for Philadelphia, and on arriving took up quarters at the United States Hotel.]

In all probability, Blackburn's boat trip from Baltimore to Philadelphia followed a route from Chesapeake Bay through the Chesapeake and Delaware Canal and up the Delaware River. Situated on the confluence of the Delaware and the Schuylkill, fifty miles inland from the head of Delaware Bay and 100 miles from the Atlantic Ocean, the city maintained the features drafted by its founder, William Penn—proportionately regular, conforming to the checkerboard or gridiron pattern, with Market and Broad streets as the main thoroughfares. Frontage on the Delaware River accommodated foreign and domestic water-borne freight. At this time Philadelphia had lost its position as the largest municipal center in the nation to New York; yet from the outset the city was noted as a leading cultural center, possessing various societies of art and science, sustained by a population of approximately 70,000 or more. The Chestnut Street and Walnut Street Theatres were the main sources of dramatic activity, comparable to the best of New York playhouses; and the city had a tradition of circus performances dating back to Richetts' Amphitheatre in 1793.

Met with Mr. Needham of Cooke's company, a good fellow; also Mr. Woolford, Mr. Cole, and Gossin. Took a glass or two together. Walked down to Walnut Street Theatre. Introduced to old Cooke. Looked at his new stud of horses; rather shy.[45] Met with Jim Burt, who had just returned from the West Indies. Went to supper, then visited the theatre; plays, "Napoleon" and "Two Gregories," Mr. Foster playing the Emperor very well, and Bill Gates playing Gregory in the last piece funnily enough. After play, went behind. Introduced to Foster and Williams, the clown. Saw them rehearse part of "The Cataract of the Ganges," and left at twelve in company with John Gossin.

This is the first American reference I find of Henry Needham. There is a Needham listed in Andrew Ducrow's company at Astley's Amphitheatre in 1835. If this is the same man, it is likely that he, too, came over with Cooke. He worked with various organizations in the United States until at least through 1847, when he was ringmaster for Spalding's North American Circus.

George Woolford, Thomas Taplin Cooke's son-in-law, was primarily a horse drama performer who came with the troupe from England. He had made his London arenic debut in the summer of 1825 with Andrew Ducrow's company. In 1836, he moved into Cooke's stable, just prior to leaving for America. His daughter, Louisa, was destined to be the second wife of Andrew Ducrow.

William H. Cole, posturer, clown, and contor-
tionist, was another son-in-law, his wife being the
former Mary Ann Cooke. The couple remained in the
United States when the Cooke troupe returned to England. Their son, born in 1847, became the famous
American circus proprietor, William Washington
Cole.

John Gossin was a Pittsburgh born clown, first
listed by Thayer with Sickles & Co. in 1832.[46] He
was popular in the 1830s and 1840s, until he became
dissipated and broken in spirit and died of yellow fever in Natchez.

James Burt was an acrobat and clown. Thayer
has listed him as a member of the just-formed Bacon
& Derious circus. Either his engagement was a brief
one or the circus was off the road for a few weeks.
Thayer has given no routing from April 22 until
June.[47]

The play that Blackburn attended was "Napoleon Bonaparte," by J. H. Amherst. Performances
were offered from April 23 through the 27. "The
Two Gregories, or Luck in a Name, or Where Did
the Money Come From?" was a popular musical farce
by T. J. Dibdin. It was presented at the Walnut Street
Theatre on April 26 and 27.[48]

Joseph C. Foster, an English clown, came
with Cooke's troupe. He was with Ludlow & Smith's
equestrian company at the American Theatre, New
Orleans, 1840-41. The following year, he went into
circus partnership with John Robinson for two seasons.

William F. Gates (d. 1843), an American, was
a low comedian, one of the most popular ever to play
the Bowery Theatre, N.Y.C. Ludlow seemed to recall

that he began in the circus business. Indeed, Thayer listed a single item of a W. Gates & Co., a presumed successor to Frost & Co. in 1838.[49] Ludlow remembers Gates as "a quiet, unpretending man, of sound mind and manly nature, genial and well disposed to all mankind."[50]

The clown Robert "Bobby" Williams (1805?-1870), another member of the 1836 Cooke entourage, remained in the United States and connected with various circuses—among them Howes & Mabie, Rockwell & Stone, June & Titus, Spalding & Rogers, etc. He performed again with Cooke's circus on its return to America in 1860 at Niblo's Garden, N.Y.C. This was followed by engagements with Sands', Madigan's, Wheeler's and other organizations through the 1860s.

"Cataract of the Ganges; or, The Rajah's Daughter," a melodrama by William Thomas Moncrieff, was one of the most popular pieces used in horse dramas, first performed at Drury Lane under Robert Elliston's management on October 27, 1823. The pseudo-historical plot, based on the recent abolition of female infanticide amongst the tribe of the Jarejahs in India, involved the concealment of the sex of his daughter by the Rajah of Guzerat. While he was away at war, a powerful rival, the Grand Brahmin of Mokarra, arranged the marriage of this bogus "Prince" to the daughter of the Emperor of Delhi. This leads to the melodramatic sequences of an equestrian bridal procession, the revelation of Zamine's true sex, and her being carried off by Mokarra with intentions of sacrificing her at the temple of Juggernaut, etc. etc.[51]

Blackburn's "old Cooke" was Thomas Taplin Cooke (1782-1866), the son of Thomas Cooke, the English circus pioneer. He brought his circus to America in 1836, which included forty members of his family—seven sons, five daughters, and a parcel of grand-children. James and George Cooke were the principal equestrians; William Cooke, the gymnast and leaper; Alfred Cooke, the slack-rope performer; Henry Cooke, the acrobat and tightrope walker; Thomas Cooke, Jr., the ringmaster. The troupe also included Woolford and Cole, Mary Anne Cole, the clowns John Wells and Robert Williams, and a Polish Brothers act. There was a stud of thirty or forty of the finest horses ever imported to this date—some full-blooded Arabians and a number of small Burmese ponies.

It was inevitable that the Cooke company would be compared to that of James West's, who brought his circus from England in 1816. Durang thought that the Cooke performances lacked the "grand effects" of West's repertory of "Timour the Tartar," "Cataract of the Ganges," etc.[52]

Cooke's performances were better suited for juvenile amusements. He introduced dramatic scenes on horse-back. The old English nursery tales were represented by children and their guardians, and there were many other little conceits of that kind. These entertainments were of a novel character, and pleased the respectable order of our society, who made the arena for a season quite a fashionable resort.

Cooke's equestrian company, which Ireland assessed as "the most complete and extensive affair of the kind yet seen in America," arrived in New York City on November 20, 1836, on the chartered ship

Roger Stewart.[53] Four days later, they opened an engagement at Vauxhall Garden, Broadway and Grand Street, where they performed until mid-February. They then moved to the Bowery Theatre for manager William Dinneford.

After the old Bowery burned in 1836, Thomas Hamblin had leased the ground on which it stood to Dinneford, who replaced and refitted the building, and opened it to the public for the first time, January 2, 1837. It was there where Cooke's company performed for some twenty nights, before closing on March 15 and making an initial appearance at the National Theatre (formerly the Italian Opera House) on March 25. Following their New York appearances, the company went to Boston, and then moved back to the Bowery for another twenty nights before their Philadelphia stand. In Philadelphia, Cooke erected an amphitheatre on Chestnut Street, east of Ninth, a building of stone and brick that seated 2,000, Cooke's Extensive Equestrian Establishment and New Arena. It was completed and opened to the public on August 28, 1837. The season continued until December 20; after which, the company moved to the Front Street Theatre, Baltimore, and opened on December 28. The engagement went well for about six weeks until the early hours of February 3, when the building was demolished by fire. Everything was lost, including the fine stud of horses which Cooke had brought with him from England. Having no insurance, he was ruined.

The entertainment world was shocked by the disaster. Thomas Hamblin, who had undergone a similar conflagration, gave Cooke his spotted horse, Mazeppa. The proprietors of Fogg & Stickney's cir-

cus in Cincinnati gave him a free benefit; as did
Charles H. Bacon, whose troupe was also performing
in Baltimore at the time.

Somewhat recovered, Cooke returned to the
amphitheatre in Philadelphia on March 12 with a stud
of American horses and an added dramatic corps, but
remained there only until the 26th. For whatever rea-
son, the company moved to the Walnut Street Theatre
and opened on April 2, 1838. The run came to an end
on May 5. After an unfortunate year and a half since
he sailed from Greenock, Scotland, on September 8,
1836, Thomas Taplin Cooke returned to his native
England.

*I met with quite an adventure coming out of
the back door. Found two women standing there, very
mysteriously waiting for two of the grooms. Was quite
astonished to find that one of them was the wife of a
particular friend of mine, an equestrian in the South.
She vanished very quickly on finding that I was in the
party. This verified the old adage of "when the cat's
away the mice will play." O woman! woman! you are
damned queer furniture. Called at a tavern and had a
snorter and a long talk. Gossin made up his mind that
he would accompany us to England, and join us for
that purpose to-morrow.*[54]

*[The ensuing day he departed for New York,
and at "Brad Jones'" in the Bowery, he met Cony and
Blanchard, whom he designated as "the committee;"
also Jack Whittaker and Levi. They "drank champagne, in the evening visited the Franklin Theatre,
where Cony and Blanchard were playing." Sunday,
Buckley & Rockwell's Circus had arrived in town,*

and he mentions as members of the company Alex Downie, Howard Sanford and John Nathans.]

Blackburn probably means John Whittaker (d. 1847), the rider, who made his debut with Price & Simpson in 1824. I believe this is the same man who was with Winfield Scott's army in Mexico in the battle of Vera Cruz, March 29, 1847. While recovering from a wound, he died of yellow fever contracted in the camp. His last words were reported to have been, "Boys, I've rode my last act. It was my best engagement and my last. Give always your horse a loose rein, but never desert your flag." It sounds like a curtain line from a bad melodrama.

Downie and Nathans are well recognized circus performers. Alexander Downie (1806-1843) was an experienced rider, clown, and trampoline performer at this time. With Aaron Turner's circus in 1820 he executed the feat of somersaulting from a horse going at full speed. A very popular entertainer, he once threw eighty somersaults without stopping. John J. Nathans (1814-1891) was one of the first to carry a child above his head as a four-horse rider. He continued to perform or be connected with circuses in one capacity or another almost until his death.

I only find Howard Sandford as a single entry by Thayer. He was a singer of comic songs with the Yeaman Circus, 1833. Thayer indicates that Matthew Buckley and Henry Rockwell were equestrians with Cooke's 1837-38 winter season. After which, with menagerie proprietor H. Hopkins, they formed Buckley, Rockwell, Hopkins & Co. Poughkeepsie was their opening date, May 1-2.[55]

[On Monday, April 30, he engaged passage for himself and North for England on board the ship Hibernia, Captain Cobb.] A fine ship and a good fellow. Took a stroll. Saw Buckley & R.'s company off for Poughkeepsie. Visited Museum; saw the Irish Giant O'Clancy, White-haired Lady, also Mr. Davison, glass-blower, all of whom Mr. Page brought out from Liverpool.[56]

Tuesday, May 1. Great day in New York for moving; everybody out of doors, bed and baggage. Afraid of being run over by carts hurrying to and fro.

[On Thursday, May 3, the ship sailed, and he then writes:] Got aboard about ten a.m., in the stream about eleven, and under way for old England at twelve. Here we are, very comfortable: Mr. and Mrs. Cony, Bill Blanchard, Levi North, Mr. Price---a gentleman and writer with whom I became acquainted in Cincinnati, Mr. Stevens, Ferguson and myself.

[Out at sea the next day is the significant entry:] No one at dinner but the Captain and myself.

Sunday, May 6. Mr. Price read prayers to the steerage passengers. Shaved Cony; only cut him in two places. Shaved myself with same success.

Friday, May 11. Made a visit to the steerage passengers. Cooking process rather slow, but they made it up in eating fast.

Sunday, May 13. Ten a.m. All hands called to prayers, the steerage passengers attending, with the exception of the Catholic portion, who had objected to the form of service. Mr. Price played the parson, and Mr. Stevens the clerk, to admiration. The cabin passengers, becoming quite moral, gave a full attendance on this occasion. One black sheep in the flock, a sacrilegious dog, stole raisins out of the pantry during *prayers. * * * * New recipe for mending black stage stockings by Mr. Price—mending them with court plaster.*[57]

> *Thursday, May 17. A row in the steerage last night between an English widow and an Irish ditto. One kicked the other out of bed. They referred the case to the captain this morning, and he decided that if they did not agree he would be obliged to put a man in bed with each of them.*

> ** * * * A quarrel between Doctor, the black cook, and Thomas, the second steward, the cook getting the best of it. "Niggers are getting ripe, by darn," vide Major Jack Downing.*

Downing was a character from Jonas B. Phillips' extravaganza, "Life in New York." It was first mounted at the Bowery Theatre in 1834 with Gates portraying the Major. Its popularity necessitated the adding of scenes, including an appearance by T. D. Rice, the famous delineator of Negro songs and burlesques, as "Jim Crow."

> ** * * * Ten p.m. Third mate Mr. Cony came below. Blanchard inquired if he had clewed up the mizzen-mast.*

> *Tuesday, May 22. One of the Irish steering passengers saw a crow, a black crow, as he said. * * * * Cony and black David cleaning out the dog kennels. Good chance for fleas to exercise themselves. * * * In removing a bale of cotton, the sailors found a rat's nest with eleven young ones, whose bodies were committed to the mighty deep. They must have thought this treatment rather salty from perfect strangers. After dinner myself and Bill Blanchard*

hove the log with Cony's water bucket, one pound of lead, fish hook, and part of a line. So much for dabbling in nautical affairs.

Blackburn in England

The England of Blackburn's day, with a population of over fifteen and a half million (1831 census), was, for all purposes, still living in the eighteenth century. It had not yet been touched by American influence; rights of laborers were not recognized; the majority of the country people could not read or write; rank and wealth were held in special reverence; and penal settlements still flourished (between 1825 and 1840, over 48,000 convicts were sent to Australia). At the same time, the country was undergoing an industrial revolution; and with it, mechanization in manufacture and travel was bringing remarkable change which would rapidly accelerate within the next fifty years. The British merchant marine was the largest and most powerful in the world. Ship-building technology was far in advance of competing nations. This very year, two paddle steamers, the *Sirius* and the *Great Western*, raced across the Atlantic in under twenty days.

Liverpool, situated on the right bank of the Mersey River, three miles from the sea, was the major port in England and the funnel for trade with the Americas. Freighters brought cotton from the docks of New Orleans, tobacco and rice from Charleston, and grain and all sorts of commercial goods from New York. Passenger travel from every direction was disembarked there. Its location, adjacent to the manufacturing centers of Lancashire, Yorkshire and the Midlands, thirty-four miles from Manchester and just less than one hundred from Birmingham, served to establish the city's importance as an export and import center. Such bustle of trade ignited a population growth from the 77,700 recorded in the 1801 census to over 370,000 in the next half-century. It was at this port of entry, Liverpool, where Captain Cobb brought his sea-weary passengers.

[Blackburn's party landed safe in Liverpool after a voyage of twenty-four days and one hour.] Went to the monument erected for Nelson. Biggest horses and carts I ever saw---one horse drawing twenty-two bales of cotton. Tell this to a Mississippian and he would laugh at you. About two, returned to the ship where I had the pleasure of being introduced to Tom Watson, a fine fellow; also Mat Robinson, a famous pugilist in this country. Took a turn up-town, visited Jim Ward, another great fighter---a large, fine looking fellow.

Tom Watson was an English clown, a member of the famous Watson family, who worked both sides of the Atlantic. He was connected with various circuses in the United States in the 1850s and 1860s.

Jem Ward was a more notable pugilist than Mat Robinson. Ward challenged Tom Cannon for the English heavyweight title in 1825. They fought in temperatures of over ninety degrees. The bout lasted only ten minutes with Ward the winner. He held the crown for a year and a half until he was challenged by Peter Crawley in 1827. Crawley won by a knockout in the eleventh round. Two days later the new champion retired from the ring. Ward reclaimed the title and retained it until 1831. On July 12, he fought the Irish champion, Simon Byrne. The fight lasted an hour and seventeen minutes with Ward coming out the winner. He announced his retirement a year later, opened a tavern, and lived to the age of eighty-one.[58]

Walked about until seven. Went to the Amphitheatre---a part of Batty's; saw a Mrs. Hughes ride--- the best female rider I ever saw. Mr. doing the Polander very well. Rest of the performance shy. Wild and Brown as clowns; Brown tolerable, Wild no go.

William Batty was an equestrian performer as early as 1828. Ten years later he had his own circus. Edward Fitzball, the writer of horse dramas, described him as a most extraordinary man, endowed with a natural intellect. After a lengthy and successful career as a showman, he died in 1868. Edwin Hughes origins' were not of the circus. He was the son of a steel toy manufacturer from Birmingham. He joined Batty's troupe and became the best polander in England, the first, it was said, to rotate a full 360 degrees on his head without holding, while balancing on a single upright spar of a come-apart ladder. He was at one time Batty's manager in Ireland. Eventually, in 1843, at the age of thirty, he formed his own company. After five years of successful operation, he retired with a handsome fortune.[59] The clowns of the circle were Henry Brown (1814-1902) and James Wild (d. 1867), minor performers when compared to some of the great English jesters.

[The next night he again visited the Amphitheatre, when he was introduced to Mrs. Hughes, who, he adds, appeared as Columbine in the panto-

mime. The show terminated at the unreasonable hour of half-past twelve. This entry ends Log No. 2.

The following day they saw Batty, who could give them but "a few days." This brief engagement was declined.]

Thursday, May 31. Shortly after breakfast, went on board the Hibernia---Mr. Cony, Mr. Stevens, Tom Watson, Levi North, Bill Blanchard and myself---for the purpose of presenting Captain Cobb with a splendid snuff box as a small token of respect we felt for his kindness extended to us on our passage. After the speech-making, the Queen, Martin Van Buren, Henry Clay, and absent friends were toasted. After returning home and dinner, Mr. and Mrs. Cony, Bill, and myself paid a visit to the St. James Cemetery, a most beautiful place of burial---a perfect paradise. Almost wanted to die. Returned home much pleased. Visited Tom Watson. A genteel fellow came in, sang, and carried round his hat for halfpennies---he wanted a club. Little boy "Jumped Jim Crow." Paid a visit to my friend Tom Grierson.

The actor, Tom Grierson, was born in Liverpool. He went to America around 1827, making his debut at the Walnut Street Theatre, Philadelphia, that year. In 1828, he appeared in N.Y.C. at the Broadway Circus. Sometime later he returned to England, where he probably remain for the rest of his life.

Friday, June 1. Got shaved by our English barber. No headpiece to the chairs. Paid threepense. [From Mr. Blackburn's diary we learn that Tom Watson was known as "The President of the Ugly Club," and he mentions drinking a pot of porter out of the

president's silver pot. Visiting the races, they take in:]
a penny Ducky---a shabby theatre, twopence admis-
sion. And such an audience I never saw---ragged
boys, coal heavers, and the lowest class of women.
On our entrance we were saluted with "Harrah for
the President of the Ugly Club!" "Bravo, Cony and
His Dogs!" "Go it, Nosey Jackson!"

Who was Nosey Jackson? Can it be that, rec-
ognizing Blackburn as an American, the shouter was
referring to Andrew Jackson, whose second term as
president had ended just two years prior and who was
well remembered in England for his overwhelming
defeat of the British forces in New Orleans, January
8, 1815, which made him a military hero of the War
of 1812?

Play not commenced, went out and took a
glass of ale. Returned. Play not yet commenced. One
of the actors drunk. Play, "Alonzo the Brave and the
Fair Imogene." Stopped to see two acts of five min-
utes' duration. Such acting I never saw before. Left
perfectly satisfied that this was the quintessence of all
exhibitions I had yet seen.

Blackburn's remarks were completely justi-
fied. The penny theatres, or sometimes called penny
"gaffs," were a form of urban entertainment for the
working class. There were some eighty to one hundred of them scattered about London alone in the
1830's, housed in converted store-fronts, barns,
sheds, or other inexpensive locations. These places
frequently seated around 200 spectators, mostly
males. Performances, consisted of comic songs, pan-

tomimes, burlesques and melodramas, the whole program lasting an average of forty-five minutes. The
actors, seldom following a written script, interacted
freely with the audience; something that came easily
to them; for, being at the bottom of their profession,
they were usually as impoverished as those who paid
to see them.[60] An 1838 account of one these places
portrays the audience as a "dirty, ragged set, principally consisting of boys and girls; two of them were
barefooted, and had scarce a rag to cover them, and
did not seem to have been washed for a month." The
theatre was "of the most wretched description."
There was a temporary stage and bits of scenery. A
sign at the entrance announced "This evening's performance: 'The Spectre of the Grave'; after which, a
comic song by Mr. Ewyn; to conclude with 'The Key
of the Little Door.'"[61]

*Saturday, 2. Saw two or three women in the
streets [of] Liverpool, picking up horse manure with
their hands and putting it in their aprons. I suppose
they sell it for a living---rather ripe living, that.
[Street montebanking was evidently a novelty to him,
for he continues:] Also four tolerably genteel fellows,
two with violins, a flute, a violincello, playing
through the streets for pennies. [This was before the
"Little German Band" in our American cities. The
same night he saw two boys dancing "Jim Crow,"
with their faces blacked with soot.]*

We connect the song and dance, "Jim Crow,"
with negro minstrelsy. But this truly American entertainment form did not exist at this time; however, T.
D. Rice had already appeared at the Adelphi Theatre,
London, with his repertory of plantation songs and

his impersonation of "Jump Jim Crow," which took the British public by storm.

[En route to London by stagecoach, he says:] Changed horses at Blue Bell. Had some cheese and ale in the kitchen. Noticed the kitchens here are as clean as our parlors. [Further on in his journey:] In a small village I got the best glass of ale I have had in the country. People keeping up Whit Monday. [At Warren:] Stopped at the George Hotel.[62] *Crowds around the coach. The Leeds and Sheffield coach came in, the guard playing the valve-trumpet beautifully. Some of the country people thought Hector, Cony's dog, a white bear, and the girls admired North's long locks. [At Birmingham:] Had a row about Cony's dogs; had to pay passage for them to London. Agent, Brotherton, a damned rascal. Left, having got a bad supper, and in no good humor.*

The British looked upon coach travel far differently than Americans. The first thirty years of the nineteenth century represented the glory era of stage coaching for them. The road had an appeal to Englishmen then unlike anyone anywhere. There was an air of romance connected with it, a feeling of enthusiasm and abandonment. Later in the century, retrospective accounts by writers and artists described the pleasures of racing along at ten miles an hour, sitting atop the rumbling rigs, listening to the cracking of the whips as the coachmen commanded more speed from their equine quartet.

Improved methods of road construction made travel faster and more comfortable. Vehicles were less likely to get mired in rain-inspired muddy stretches or brake an axle from ugly ruts along the route. Coaches were constructed of lighter materials and supported more pliable springs. Thus, speed and precision became the competitive edge for rival coach lines, reflected in the names given their vehicles: "Highflyer," "Quicksilver," "Comet," "Rocket," "Greyhound."

There were stops along the way for refreshment and for overnight rest. Inns dotted the roadways every few miles. But because of the rigid schedules, there was no time for casual eating—ten minutes for breakfast, twenty minutes for dinner—before the guard's horn interrupted the repast. The assessment of the food served at these places depended on who described it. One writer referred to the usual coach dinner as "a course, fat leg of mutton, roasted to a cinder, a huge joint of boiled beef, underdone, and gritty cabbage." Another remembered his breakfast more fondly. "The table was covered with the whitest of white clothes and of china, and bore a pigeon-pie, a ham, a round of cold boiled beef; and a waiter came in with a tray of kidneys, and steaks, and eggs and bacon, and toast and muffins, and coffee and tea."[63]

Half-past ten, arrived in Coventry, celebrated for making ribbons and for Sir John Falstaff's ragged regiment; also, a certain Sleeping Tom. Coach changing horses, took a pot of ale, fancying its sack, and thinking myself Sir John in his younger days, when he could have crawled through an alderman's thumbring.

"Crawled through an alderman's thumb-ring" is a reference to the corpulent Falstaff's speech from

Shakespeare's "Henry IV, Part I," Act II, scene 4: "My own knee! when I was about thy years, Hal, I was not an eagle's talon in the waist; I could have crept into any alderman's thumb-ring: a plague of sighing and grief! it blows a man up like a bladder."

Tuesday, 5. Arrived in London. Drove to Charing Cross and put up at the Golden Cross. Called for breakfast. Could not get a room to wash or dress in. Cursed the whole fraternity of English landlords. In a devil of a pickle; tore the whole seat of my trousers across in leaping from the coach. Had to wear my coat buttoned.

Coventry was about the half-way point between Liverpool and London, which was a two-day trip. Charing Cross was the terminus for the stage line approaching London from the Coventry road. The Golden Cross has been described as a five-story brick structure of Georgian architecture with sashed shop fronts on either side of the coach entry.[64]

London was a crowded and bustling city. At the time of the 1831 census, it consisted of 14,000 acres, or nearly twenty-two square miles. Its population was roughly 1,600,000, with an estimated 12,000 visitors every year. There were 90,000 passengers going across London Bridge daily. The 1,200 cabriolets, 600 hackney coaches, and 400 omnibuses caused frequent stoppages on the busy thoroughfares.[65] The city as noisy with sounds of the night watch, milkwomen and newsmen in the early morning, chimney-sweeps and dustmen, fish venders, and all sorts of hawkers—muffin men, "buy a broom" girls, etc. Italians played hurdy-gurdies or ground out upright pianos, accompanied in entertainment by their monkeys.

How did Londoners amuse themselves? There were some fifteen theatres within the boundaries of the city. There were public bazaars for the sale of fancy articles, millinery, jewelry, etc. The Thames Tunnel, unfinished at this time, was an item of curiosity, for which the public paid a shilling to be admitted. There were numerous museums and other places of exhibition. At the lower end of St. Martin's Lane was a place where a gigantic whale, ninety-five feet long and eighteen across, could be viewed for a shilling, two shillings to sit in the whale's belly. The Zoological Gardens, at Regent's Park, opened in 1828, was the larger of two such places to house exotic birds and animals. There were gambling houses and men's clubs where gaming was tolerated—card playing, dicing and lotteries. There were horse and dog races. There were opportunities of sporting for fish and fowl, as well as fox and stag, the latter serving as an excuse for great social gatherings and the breeding of horses and hounds to intensify the sport. There were cricket matches and billiard rooms. For improving the mind and soul, there were parks and public gardens, music concerts, and art exhibits. There was Madame Tussaud's Gallery in Baker Street, the Hippodrome at Bayswater, the Diorama in Regent's Park, the Panorama in Leicester Square.

The taverns, where Londoners took their dinners and drank their grog, were plentiful. In the city there was one public eating and drinking trough to every fifty-six houses, called by such names as the "Cheshire Cheese", "The Cock," "The Coal Hole," "The Rainbow," "Clitter's," "The Albion," "The

Finish," "The Cider Cellar," "The Royal Saloon," "Piccadilly," "Offley's," "Kean's Head," and a host of others.

Beer was always the standard drink of England. Tea and coffee were too expensive for the common folk, as were cocoa and chocolate. In 1830 an act was passed to permit the sale of beer by retail, which was described by the *Times* as "a great victory obtained for the poor over the unpitying avarice of the rich."[66] This act made licenses for places selling only beer easy to obtain. Every variety of the beverage was dispensed—dark and heavy Shropshire ale, luscious Burton, mellow October, solid brown stout, new ale, old ale, hard ale, soft ale, and balmy Scotch.

The drinking of gin, or "blue ruin," was a favorite among the lower classes—the drink of women as much as of men. "Gin-shops" were no longer located solely in the dirty byways of the city. By 1834, proprietors vied for superiority of finely arranged decor by fitting their places up with rich carvings, brass work, mahogany paneling, gilding and ornamental paintings. Gin, it was stated, had become "a giant demi-god—a mighty spirit, dwelling in gaudy gold-beplastered temples," where may be seen "maudlin, unwashed multitudes, ... old men and maidens, grandsires and grandams, fathers and mothers, husbands, wives, and children, crowding, jostling, and sucking in the portions of the spirit which the flaunting priestesses dole out to them in return for their copper offerings."[67]

When Blackburn arrived in London, preparations for Victoria's coronation were already in progress. Carpenters and upholsterers were readying the ceremonial structures at Westminster Abbey. Tempo-

rary seating, running from the nave to the choir loft,
was being built for the accommodation of 1,200 of
the very special people. The procession from Buckingham House to the Abbey was being planned on a
splendid scale. The route was to pass along Constitu-
tion Hill, Piccadilly, St. James Street, Pall Mall,
Cockspur Street, Charing Cross, Whitehall and Par-
liament Street, and return again to Buckingham by the
same way. The avenues were being decorated with
flags, banners and triumphal arches. Eventually, they
would be lined with troops during the procession, and
bands would be dispersed at various locations along
the way. Near the Abbey, temporary galleries were
being erected to accommodate the common spectators. At the entrance to the great Abbey, a Gothic
porch was under construction, to be equipped with
convenient retiring and robing rooms for the Queen
and her suite. Large crowds of "respectable persons"
were gathering at the house of Mr. Edward Howe,
silk weaver in Castle Street, to observe the material
used for the Queen's robe. All England was a hubbub
of activity. The excitement that filled the air was as
thick as London's fog.

*After breakfast bribed a chambermaid with a
shilling, got a room, and dressed and shaved, and
began my peregrinations through the renowned city of
London. Cony and Stevens gone out to look for lodg-
ings; Blanchard and North walked off; I left alone in
this living wilderness---thousands of faces and not
know one. Took a walk around one square. I did not
venture any farther. Saw a regiment of foot; got lost
in looking at them. With some difficulty, found my*

way back to the Golden Cross, although I had not been fifty yards from it.

[Lodgings were found at 120 London Road, Surrey Side. Speaking of the charges, he adds:] In the United States it is dog eat dog, but here they are not so particular; it is dog eat anything. [He takes exception to the feeing of the chambermaid and "Boots."] Half-past six, visited Astley's Theatre. The first piece, "Conquest of Babylon," one of the most gorgeous and best got-up pieces I ever witnessed.[68] I never saw anything in that way half so magnificent. Next came the equestrian performance. A Mr. Clark rode the Indian---the worst man rider I ever saw; it would have been a disgrace to old Sizer's Steamboat Circus on the Mississippi. Mr. Woolford rode next, foot back all the time, and rest made up with different positions with a wreath. Miss Ducrow, a girl about seven years old, road very well with a cat gut string attached to her waist, run down through the pommel, and so on to the ringmaster's hand, who, by the bye, was a nigger. Next came Mr. Price, the greatest vaulter in the world---said to be---and one of the clowns, for they had four this night. Rather shy, ain't scared yet. He has done thirty-one somersaults. Did at four trials thirteen. He would be rather bad shaped among the Yankees.

Andrew Ducrow, with William West as a partner, had taken the management of Astley's in 1830, where he exhibited his genius for *mise-en-scene*. Ducrow's hippo dramatic compositions often consisted of civil, religious and military processions combined with an almost uninterrupted series of combats, single and double, in sets of six, eight and ten, on foot and horseback, as well as terrific engagements of whole battalions, and even armies, all of which displayed a liberal amount of killed and wounded. The number of people employed at one time by him during his management was said to have exceeded one hundred and fifty. His weekly expenses were seldom less than five hundred pounds.[69] Still, Ducrow had a contempt for the literary parts of the drama. Being illiterate, he rarely attempted speaking roles. His favorite comment while arranging scripts for the arena was, "Cut the dialect (dialogue) and come to the 'osses."[70]

Miss Ducrow was probably Louisa Margaret Foy Wood, daughter of Ducrow's sister, and a great favorite of Andrew. The ringmaster, John Esdaile Widdecombe (1787-1854), billed as "Methuselah," had been with the Amphitheatre before Ducrow's arrival. He was said to be the most noted master of the circle in the history of Astley's or any other circus, his fame being the result of his carefully contrived appearance and conduct—"from the scented curl of his southern brow to the elaborate splendour of his French-polished boot."[71] But Blackburn has confused the ringmaster with a Cossack rider and pupil of Ducrow's, Joseph Hillier, who was a Negro or a mulatto. As one jester spoke it, "Hillier has ridden until he has become black in the face." Mr. Clark may have been John Clarke (1786?-1864), equestrian, clown, and circus proprietor, who originated Dick Turpin's famous ride to York on the equestrian stage. He was descendant of a long line of English circus people. Sizer was an American provincial showman of little record. The very thorough Thayer noted he had a steamboat circus in 1838, but admits knowing nothing of the man personally.[72] Thomas Price, listed on the bills as the "Antipodean Wonder," or "the Bouncing Ball," was new to the company this season. This man, who claimed to have thrown fifty-six somersaults, one after another, will soon become prominent within our narrative.

Last of all came the renowned Ducrow, the great, the wonderful. Rode an act called "Figaro."[73] *He pantomimed well, first-rate; but he has been overrated unmercifully as a rider. He never was the rider that North is. He tried to make a finish to his act; his attitudes were all incorrect, and in throwing off he pointed his heel as much as any rider I ever saw come from the mill at Somerstown, where they make 'em.*[74] *In fact, he in his time has stuck a horse well---all dash and splash, but he never was a Herr Cline for grace. So much for my first impression of Mr. D. as a rider.*

Blackburn's criticism of Ducrow is unfair. Even though he was past his peak and waning in vigor, Ducrow was, as someone put it, the inventor of histories on horseback. His equestrian poses and dances were exquisite exhibitions of classic grace and artistic imagination. The flat of a horse's back was his stage, from which he created a style of performance copied by many of the young riders of his day. His skills in the precise movements of dressage and *haute ecole* are well confirmed. In the more traditional field of equitation, he was also conceded to be an expert.

And, oh, Andre Cline! What an artist on the tight rope he was, this Englishman who preferred the German moniker of "Herr," and who performed with such grace and eloquence. He first appeared in America at the Bowery Theatre, N.Y.C., 1828; and continued performing in both theatres and equestrian arenas, in America and abroad, well into the 1860's.

> *The entertainment finished with a grand spectacle in honor of the young Queen, which was really very beautiful. I forgot to mention a pony, the best broken I ever saw; did tricks I could not imagine a horse could be taught. The play was out about eleven. Dropped into The Pheasant, a great resort for the equestrians. Got a pot of ale and a pipe. Introduced to old Tom Blanchard, the great Pantaloon, father of Bill, a jolly, smart old fellow.*
>
> *Wednesday, 6. Levi and myself started to see the great Monsieur Ducrow. On the road fell in with Mr. Ellar, the famous Harlequin.*

Tom Blanchard was a Pantaloon at Covent Garden in 1827. His last appearance in the character was at the Victoria Theatre in 1845. He also had established a reputation as a skilled broadswordsman. Old Tom died in London on August 20, 1859, age 72. Tom Ellar was one of the many great Harlequins. He performed in that role when the first English pantomime was taken to Paris in 1825. He was said to have "a curious art of spinning his head round with remarkable velocity as if the masked face was only a whirling teetotum revolving in the centre of his frilled neck." Eventually Ellar declined from stardom to seedy music halls and then to the gutter, which inspired Thackeray to observe that the "prince of many enchanted islands, was the law-breaker for acting at a penny theatre after having well-nigh starved in the streets where nobody would listen to his old guitar. No one gave him a shilling to bless him, not one of us who owe him so much. So passes the glory of Harlequin." The poor man died in 1840, following a benefit performance at the Victoria Theatre.[75]

Arrived at the Amphitheatre, rang the bell, servant came down, sent up my letter of introduction, invited up. There we sat in his great Mogulship's presence. Had a talk with him and arranged to come and try the board in the afternoon. Well you may talk about circus riders living, but if he don't live like a prince I'm a dogfish. He lays back in the shade, with his morning gown on, biggest kind of an armchair, more mahogany sideboards, silver plates and marble statues. He took us into his best room. I expect he thought he would scare us at the start.

Came up to the Surrey Theatre. Met Ben Stickney. Glad to see us. Went home to dine with him.

Benjamin Stickney, the brother of S. P. Stickney (father of a famous brood of American circus performers) and John H. Stickney, was noted for his usefulness in horse dramas. He spent a large part of his career performing in England.

[Going to the Amphitheatre at two o'clock, they found it too late to try the board; so made up a party consisting of Levi North, Cony, Blanchard, Stevens and old Tom Blanchard to visit the fair in Greenwich in a "go-cart."] The shows were the greatest curiosity; more to be seen outside than in. Richardson's booth was our first. [He died some weeks ago worth forty thousand pounds. It is now managed by Nelson

Lee.] On the platform in front, they had Harlequin, Clowns, Pantaloons, Columbines, men doing contortioning and tumbling, all kinds of tragedy chaps, a pretty good exhibition outside, with a band of twelve musicians. Paid sixpence each and went inside. Saw part of a tragedy, and left to see the other wonderments.

Passed old Saunders' show. Jim Hunter served his time there. Price of admission only one penny. Dancing and tumbling outside. Dropped into Clarke's to see the riders.[76] Price sixpence. Performance about twenty minutes long---little boy and girl rode; three young men in contortions, very good; and finished with Billy Button. Opened the back door and let folks out, while others came in at the front. Introduced to old Clarke, who said Matt Buckley served time with him.

John Richardson died in 1836. Lee (1806-1872), the son of a naval officer, took to the stage early in life and became a juggler with a traveling company. He developed into an actor, performing Clown, Pantaloon, and Harlequin, the latter at the Surrey Theatre in 1834. After, at various times, managing the Marylebone, Sadler's Wells, and Standard theatres, he entered into a partnership for the proprietorship of the City of London Theatre, with which he was connected for fifteen years. Later in life, he had a hand in managing the Crystal Palace Theatre.[77]

Richardson's booth was recorded in 1825 as accommodating more than a thousand people, where standing room was the general state of affairs. Outside, an elevated platform, lined at the back with green drapes and ornamented with hundreds of lamps of various colors, served to "bally" the entertainment within. The noise of the uniformed band drew the crowds, before which the members of the company promenaded around the stage in full costume. "Just a-going to begin! Pray come for'erd, come for'erd!" was the cry. The company advertised a change of performance each day, "an entire new melodrama," concluding with a "New Comic Harlequinade, with New Scenery, Tricks, Dresses, and Decorations." Charles Dickens described a performance of Richardson's show at Greenwich Fair as a melodrama with three murders and a ghost, a pantomime, a comic song, an overture, and some incidental music, all done in five-and-twenty minutes.[78] The great actor, Edmund Kean, was one of the many who got their start with John Richardson's fair show. In addition to performing in the pantomimes and melodramas, Kean gave Shakespearean recitals to audiences much like those who stood in the pit of the old Globe Theatre in Elizabethan times.[79]

Greenwich Fair was similar to the several other annual pleasure festivals—Stourbridge, Southwark, Bartholomew, *et al*, where rides, stalls, and show booths were lined up, side-by-side, much like our present day carnival midways. In 1837, Bartholomew Fair was described as "a scene of unbridled profligacy, licentiousness, and drunkenness, with fighting, both of fists and cudgels, pumping on pickpockets, robbery and cheating, noise and shouting, the braying of trumpets and the banging of drums."[80]

Abraham Saunders (1747?-1839) began his circus proprietorship in the latter part of the eighteenth century and continued well over fifty years. He got his training as an equestrian and rope-dancer at

the original Astley's Amphitheatre. While his show
was at Bartholomew Fair in 1801, one his performers, a young man named Carey, fell while conducting
a tumbling act as a monkey. This ended the circus
career of the great Edmund Kean. The Jim Hunter
referred to is the English equestrian from Astley's
Amphitheatre, who was recruited and brought to
America by Stephen Price in 1822 to become the first
real bareback riding star in this country. He returned
to England in 1829 and performed in fairs and other
cheap events. One day, in a drunken spree, he stole a
coat from Ben Stickney and, for this offense, he was
tried, convicted and sentenced to the penal colony in
Australia. It is true that Matthew B. Buckley, rider,
general performer, and showman, began as a clown at
English fairs. Price and Simpson brought him to
America in 1826, where he was connected with many
circuses as well as managing his own. He was the father of Harry, Edward and Page Buckley.

*[Blackburn relates an amusing incident of
their homeward trip. They hired a carriage and:]
Came home at a pretty good jog. Driver too smart for
Stevens, who gave him a shilling. Driver told Stevens
he had made a mistake and given him a sovereign.
Stevens gave him another shilling for his honesty. After he had gone, Stevens found his sovereign-brass.
The fellow had palmed a George the Fourth medal on
him. Supper, and went to Davis' tap. Pot of half-and-
half and a screw of tobacco. Saw the master carpenter of the Victoria Theatre. Engaged him to make a
vaulting board.*

This was the old Cobourg Theatre, re-christened in 1833, as a result of then Princess Victoria visiting there. It served for some years as a house of melodrama. "The lower orders rush there in mobs," wrote the prominent actor Charles Mathews, "and, in shirt sleeves, applaud frantically, drink ginger-beer, munch apples, crack nuts, call the actors by their Christian names, and throw them orange-peel and apples by way of bouquets."

[While waiting for the completion of the vaulting board, frequent walks and talks were taken, and frequent references made to Ben Stickney.]

Saturday, 9. Something new, a large wagon traveling continually over the city---you pay a certain sum for the privilege of sticking bills on it. [An incident of the next Sunday:] During dinner a man commenced a sermon in the street opposite our window. But it was no go; he could not gather a crowd, and gave it up as a bad job. So he walked away, thinking like many a poor theatrical after playing to a bad house, that it was not his bad acting, but entirely owing to the corrupted taste of the people.

Tuesday, 12. [He speaks of meeting with Deaf Burke, the great fighting man of England, at his favorite resort, Davis' tap.] Burke speaks very highly of the United States, but damns the Irish on account of the affair at New Orleans.

James "Deaf" Burke was Jem Ward's successor as champion of England. Shortly after he assumed the title, a fight at St. Albans between Burke and Simon Byrne changed the course of his career. The bout lasted ninety-eight rounds. The two battled for three hours and sixteen minutes, the longest championship fight on record. Byrne died from the beating he took. Disconsolate over the affair, Burke went into retirement. Shortly, Samuel O'Rourke, who became the Irish title holder after Byrne's death, threw out a challenge; but Burke refused the fight when O'Rourke insisted on the match being held in Ireland, realizing that feelings were still running high from the Byrne tragedy.

With few opponents available, O'Rourke sailed for America. Arriving in New York City, he let it be known that Burke was afraid to fight him. Meanwhile, Burke was unable to get major fights at home because of lingering public revulsion; so he too left for the United States, arriving in New York in February of 1834, ready to accept O'Rourke's challenge. But the Irishman was no longer there. He had moved to New Orleans and opened a tavern, which became a favorite haunt of longshoremen, sailors and various kinds of hoodlums. And from his southern citadel, safely surrounded by his entourage of toughs and sons of Erin, O'Rourke announced in the newspapers his claim of the "championship of the world" and offered to fight anyone for a side bet of one thousand dollars. Meanwhile, while O'Rourke was "the peacock" of New Orleans, Burke was encountering difficulty in obtaining anything but small-money exhibition fights. On hearing of O'Rourke's challenge, he raised a portion of the bet money and set sail for New Orleans.

The match was arranged, the ring set up on a site outside of New Orleans, and the crowd gathered. The host of onlookers was composed of "fashionable Creoles, French gamblers, half-breeds, Yankee sharps, Irish toughs, and smugglers and picaroons from the Barataria swamps and lakes." Both fighters came with their army of supporters, flashing pistols, bowie knives, and clubs.

The brawl began as one might expect, with insults being thrown from all sides. In the third round, Burke closed O'Rourke's right eye with two hammer blows. With that, one of O'Rourke's cornermen sprang at Burke with a bowie knife. Burke turned on him and, with one punch, put him on his back. At once, O'Rourke's infuriated thugs surrounded Burke with intentions of murder. Realizing the danger, Burke flailed his way through the crowd and fled into a wooded area, where one of his backers had a horse standing ready for such an emergency. Coincidentally, the man was James Caldwell, owner of the St. Charles Theatre. Burke wasted no time. He sped back to the city, across Canal Street, down Camp Street, and directly to the theatre. There he dismounted, burst through the stage door, and ran onto the stage of the St. Charles, where he interrupted Junius Brutus Booth in a rehearsal of "Hamlet." He was taken to Booth's dressing room until police arrived, then spirited out of town on a Mississippi steamer for St. Louis and safety.[81] This melodramatic encounter is what Blackburn referred to in his dairy: that Burke still "damns the Irish on account of the affair in New Orleans."

On his return from America, Burke took a benefit at the New Shooting Gallery, Saville Place, Leicester Square, on June 11. In addition to a demonstration of sparring, he exhibited his imitations of Venetian Statues, begowned in appropriate costumes. And, with a keen sense of the theatrical, he threw down his American championship belt as a symbolic challenge for the championship of England.

[During the waiting for the vaulting board, Mrs. Cony had gone to housekeeping, and the "American colony," with the exception of Stevens, so often referred to, had taken up residence with the Conys. On the 12th he writes:] Mr. Moles brought the board home shortly after dinner. Could not get it through the entry. Brought it through the front and back windows into the garden. Fixed it up. Levi tried it; did not do very well. Did sixteen on it. Myself and Blanchard made garden. Levi tried the board again before supper with the same success. After supper visited the Garrick Theatre. Much pleased with Bill Wood's playing of the mute in a new piece of much interest, called "Dumb Man of Manchester;" his acting was very beautiful---the best pantomime acting I ever witnessed. Met with a brother of little Harry Lewis. This is the first time I ever went to a theatre in the daylight and had the daylight to come home in. The nights are very short here, a little past one when the play was out, and the day breaking.

The Garrick Theatre was built in Leman Street, Whitechapel, in 1830. It always held a low position and had difficulty attracting responsible management. It was probably at this time that performances were given twice daily, much like a "penny show." Befitting of the place, Bill Wood was a performer of the same mold as Cony and Blanchard. The play that Blackburn attended, "Dumb Man of Manchester," was a melodrama by B. F. Rayner.

Harry Lewis was the son of the noted British actor, William T. "Gentleman" Lewis. Harry, who left England in 1835 to perform in America, was a poor imitation of his father, on the stage and off.

Wednesday, 13. After breakfast Levi tried the board again. Could not do over sixteen or seventeen somersaults. Found out that the board was too long, making it tremble in "beating it," which caused it to counter-beat. Levi went to see Mr. Moles to have it altered. Deaf Burke came to dine with us. Burke, Blanchard, Cony and myself hired a wherry to see a boat race from Westminster Bridge to Putney Bridge, a distance of seven miles. Away we went up the river at a rapid rate, Burke and Cony pulling, myself and Bill looking on. [A glowing description of the sights along the Thames follows, and an animated account of the race between the two eight-oared crews is given. They got a ducking in a pouring rain, and arrived home like drowned rats. On the return, Cony and Blanchard pulled at the oars:] Burke amusing me with songs. He sings like a raven.

Thursday, 25.[82] *Levi improving; did twenty-five. [It appears by several entries in the log that Price had already become jealous of North, the Yankee stranger, and proceeded to imitate the newcomer's vaulting board.]*

It is important to clarify the type of vaulting which will form the manner of contest between North and Price. The art of vaulting was carried to its extreme in the nineteenth century through feats of perilously long somersaulting jumps over animals or other obstacles. The performer ran down a ramp at high

speed to where an ash or hickory springboard served
as a catapult to propel the leap. The foot and a half
wide ramps varied in length depending on the nature
of the event, some extending for over fifty feet, with
inclines of from as much as ten feet at the top de-
scending to some five or six feet where it met the
springboard. Each performer took his turn in attempts
to outdo the other in height, distance, and stamina,
turning one or two somersaults before alighting on
straw-filled mats placed at the far end. The ultimate
occurred with the lining together of innumerable
horses, elephants and other objects to create a pyra-
mid effect, the degree of difficulty increasing with
each successive jump. The competitive nature of this
type of performance served to enhance audience interest and to develop super stardom, box office appeal, for the athletes involved. This was probably the
most dangerous act within the 19th century circus
program.[83] Many were the leapers who lost their lives
as they misjudged their flight and landed upside-
down, breaking their necks.

It appears that the North and Price contests
were not examples of distance and height, but, rather,
tests of endurance. The competitors bounced on a
springboard, turned a somersault, and landed on a
mattress placed in the ring. It is unclear as to whether
or not they ran down a ramp to accomplish their
leaps. Achievement was judged by the number of successive somersaulting jumps thrown by each performer. Considering the repetitive nature of the event,
one must assume that without the competitive element
within the act the spectators could easily lose interest.
The use of clowns, supporting each contestant, urging

the crowd on and capering in the arena between vaults, created an additional element of interest.

Thursday, 14. Walked as far as Astley's. Price has got two bars to his board. Levi saw Mr. Broadfoot, Ducrow's agent. Wanted us to come a week on trial. No go. Mr. Ducrow out of town, keeping his honeymoon, having been married last Sunday to Miss Woolford. We see him next Monday about engagement. In the evening, Levi and myself went to the Amphitheatre. A Miss Lee rode much better than Miss Woolford. A new Christmas entree, very beautiful. Stickney rode two horses, carrying the boy very well. Went into the famed long room at Astley's, a perfect sight for an equestrian. Looked like a fair, undressing.

William D. Broadfoot also performed in the ring spectacles and stage managed them when Ducrow was ill or otherwise occupied. He was married to Ducrow's sister, Emily. His temperament must have been similar to his employer's, for he was known as "the great swearer," because of his conduct when things were going badly. A. Y. Broadfoot, William's brother, also worked for Ducrow in some minor capacity.

The "Miss Woolford" was Louisa Woolford, daughter of Robert Woolford and sister of George, who in 1828, at age 14, had made her debut with Ducrow's company. She was described at that time as "a very attractive and promising young lady." Within the next ten years, she developed into a popular arenic attraction, second only to Ducrow himself.[84] The death of Ducrow's wife, Margaret, in January of

1837, opened the way for the marriage of Louisa and Andrew, an event which occurred on June 10, 1838.

The Miss Lee would be Rosina Lee, who made her debut as one of Ducrow's infant performers around 1827, billed as "La Petite Lee." One of her numbers in the 1838 production was called "The Greek Maid."

[On Tuesday next he:] Did not go out all day. Jack Johnson called and read one act of play he is writing for Cony. Levi tried board; did twenty-eight, and tore his trousers.

[The entry for Sunday gives a pretty domestic picture:] Cony and Jack Johnson gone sailing on the Thames; Bill out on a private visit; Levi writing letter to Ned Derious; Mrs. Cony sewing window curtains; Ann, the servant girl, preparing dinner; David scouring the knives; old Bruin asleep in his kennel; and I writing journal. Deaf Burke came to dinner.

Monday, 18. A Mr. Gilbert came to see Cony, a young actor who had acted with him in America. Deaf Burke accompanied him. [The next evening he again visited Astley's.][85] Saw Mr. Hicken ride "The Sailor." Think he is the best I have seen yet. Finished with "The Battle of Waterloo." Have seen it done better in America.

Edward Hicken (1802-1887), who, with Hillier and Stickney, were the principal male riders, had joined Ducrow in 1837. Prior to that, he was with Ryan's circus in Birmingham. The sailor act Blackburn refers to was Ducrow's "Vicissitudes of a Tar," but Hicken rode it under the title "A Tale of the Sea."

"The Battle of Waterloo" was written by J. H. Amherst. It incorporated all the spectacle of color, costume, military maneuvering, and horsemanship one could imagine in a single piece. Each act ended with a "general contest" of horse and foot. There was a Grand Entry of the French military, including Napoleon himself; a soldier was dragged off with one foot in the stirrup; Prussian infantrymen were rescued from drowning; a commander's horse was shot from under him; the Duke of Wellington conducted a Grand Review; cannons roared; colors were floated in triumph; a town went up in flames; and volleys of Roman candles flashed about. In short, the expanse of the entire field of battle was condensed into the space of Astley's oval.[86]

Wednesday, 20. Went to the Victoria to see Hart's new piece, "Mary Le Moor"---a fine piece, and well played. Oxberry played a cockney to admiration.

Thursday, 21. After breakfast, walked to the Amphitheatre. Met with Price, Bullock the clown, and Stickney.[87] Price showed his snuff box. Almost a young coffin, and a medal nearly large enough for a coffin plate, which he received for doing thirty-one somersaults. Coming home saw three men singing and begging in the streets; called themselves "poor farmer boys"---each about forty years of age! Jack Johnson dined with us and read a new piece he had been writing for Blanchard---very good. After dinner, Cony, Jack and myself visited the King's Bench Prison, a large and comfortable place of confinement for debtors. Quite a little town, a walled city in miniature--- shoemaker, tailor, barber and other shops, two tav-

*erns, fine ground for exercise, ball alleys, etc. You
would hardly call it confinement. Witnessed a sack
race, which was very amusing.*

During this period, people unable or unwilling
to pay their debts could be arrested and imprisoned at
the suit of anyone to whom they owed money. The
Imprisonment for Debt Act of 1827 mandated that the
debt be in excess of £20. The offender was released
upon complete restitution. In contrast to general prisoners, debtors enjoyed certain advantages. Their
families were allowed to accompany them into their
incarceration, they could entertain visitors, and could
bring in certain items, such as tobacco and other sun-
dries. Each debtor paid rent according to his status
and the privileges he and his family received. Queen's
Bench was famous for the latitude allowed its residents. Drinking, smoking and roistering were a
nightly pastime at its Brace Tavern, where the best
stout in the city was to be had.

In London there were three establishments set
aside for housing such truants: Marshalsea, Fleet, and
Queen's Bench Prison. According to a late 18th century report, Queen's Bench, bounded by St. George's
Fields, Blackman Street, and Borough High Street,
consisted of a coffee house, a tap house and several
structures for lodging and servicing the prisoners.
The whole place was enclosed with a wall about thirty
feet in height. King's Bench was burned by rioters in
1780, but the rebuilding was similar to what has just
been described.[88]

It was said that the debtors' prisons belonged
to the great middle class. The "villainous ghost" of
insolvency or bankruptcy "seized its victims by the

collar and hauled them within the walls of a Debtors' Prison, where it made them abandon hope, and abide there till the day of death."[89]

> *Went to Davis' and met Bullock the clown and Mr. Benedict, a chorus singer at the St. Charles Theatre, New Orleans, in 1836.*
> *After tea, Levy and myself took a cab to Vauxhall Gardens, an enchanting place, beautiful beyond description.*

Vauxhall Gardens opened its 1838 season on June 13, with admission prices being lowered to one shilling. A "magnificent" new building had been erected at the site of the old firework tower for the purpose of launching the monstrous Nassau balloon. The walks had been re-graveled and the buildings newly painted and embellished. At the termination of the principal walk, an allegorical representation of Neptune rising from the ocean astride a decorative shell and drawn by five marine horses replaced the statuary formerly resting on the site.

Vauxhall Gardens was one of the great 18th century outdoor amusements. After Jonathan Tyers acquired the gardens in 1728, he developed them into a favorite summer meeting place. Everyone went to the Gardens, the rich and the poor, the respectable and those who were not. Londoners from all walks of life congregated on the grounds to listen to the musical concerts, to dance, enjoy the shady nooks or repose in the soft illumination of the evening gas lights and wander along the flowery paths.[90] There was dining in the painted arbors where one feasted on Vauxhall ham—"sliced cobwebs"; Vauxhall beef—"book

muslin, pickled and boiled"; and heavens! that wonderful Vauxhall punch. There were fireworks and
rope dancing and balloon ascensions. Indeed, there
was something for everyone and everyone for something.

Formerly called Foxhall or Spring Garden, the
place opened about the middle of May and closed at
the end of August, with the public being admitted
only on Mondays, Wednesdays and Fridays throughout that period. The concerts commenced at 8:00
p.m. At the peak of popularity, daily attendance ran
between 5,000 and 15,000. The gardens' hey-day
was from 1750 to 1790, after which the place went
into a slow decline, surviving until 1859 when the
grounds were sold.

*The first thing on entering the enclosure is a
splendidly illuminated, covered walk around three
sides of a square some hundred feet in extent; the
lamps, which amounted to some seven or eight million, of variegated colors, forming different devices---
coat-of-arms, flags, festoons. And in the center of the
square stood a beautiful temple of the Grecian order,
about fifty feet in height, covered with lamps repre-
senting a temple of fire. Emerging from the square
were the walks, winding through all parts of the garden, rows of lamps and hundreds of beautiful statues
on either side. At the end of one of the walks was a
beautiful jet d'eau of Neptune drawn by five sea
horses, the water flying from their nostrils and his
trident to a great height, forming the most imposing
group of statuary I ever saw. In passing around the
different walks the attention is attracted by a great
variety of artificial scenes, which appear almost natu-*

ral, such as "The Cave of the Hermit," the fire burning cheerfully, and "The Monk at His Devotions," with the moon shining very naturally through the window of an old abbey. About eight p.m. a large bell was rung, to notify the visitors of the commencement of the different performances which were to take place during the evening. They began with a beautiful waltz, played by a full military band in the temple. Their places were then taken by a full orchestra, which played a grand overture; after which four songs by four different gentlemen and one by a lady---all sang finely. The bell rang again. Following the crowd, we were brought up to the Rotunda Theatre, a very pretty theatre, capable of holding two thousand persons. The performances here commenced with a young man playing two airs on the accordion, which he did exquisitely. I never thought the instrument could be brought to such perfection. He was followed by a lady on the harp, accompanied by a man playing on his chin, who executed very rapidly. Next came a play, in which Mr. Buckingham gave some excellent impersonations of Kean and Mathew's; which were done excellently well if I could judge by the applause bestowed upon him. The entertainment at the Rotunda terminated with a new style of statues after Canova by two men, three women and one child. This was the most beautiful exhibition it has been my lot to witness, especially the statues of "The Graces" by the women. With such exquisite forms, dressed in white tights, giving them the appearance of marble, a person could hardly imagine they were real flesh and blood. Bell rang again, bringing us to the "Thalian Walk," five hundred feet in length, at the end of which were two fine statues of Napoleon and Wellington. The next ex-

hibition was the Ballet Theatre, where four splendid panoramic scenes were exhibited, one of the rising sun at sea was really grand. The whole affair terminated at eleven p.m. with one of the most magnificent displays of fireworks I ever beheld. Got home at half-past eleven, well satisfied with the excursion; and so cheap, too---only one shilling. It was, as the old saying goes, "rather too much pork for a shilling."

[This ends Log No. 4.]

Sunday, 24. [He refers to preparations going on for the coronation of the Queen, and adds:] Dined with Stickney at his brother-in-law's, a Mr. Scott, dry-goods merchant, Westminster Road.

Monday, 25. Did not go out till night. Went to Victoria Theatre. Cony and Blanchard's first appearance since their return from America. Bill played the Ourang-Outang well; was called out by the audience and made a speech. Cony played the Cherokee Chief well, with great applause, and was called for at the finish of the entertainment. Concluded with "The Sprig of Laurel," a Mr. Hall playing Nipperkin the worse kind.

Perhaps the unfortunate Mr. Hall in O'Keefe's farce, "The Rival Soldiers, or The Sprigs of Laurel," was the Harry Hall who made his American debut in 1855. Ireland states the he was "an actor of good repute from London" but that he "gained no permanent position on the New York stage."[91] Score another for Blackburn's critical judgment. Hall died in Cincinnati three years after his New York arrival at the age of fifty.

Got home at half-past two. Mrs. C. rather in a bad humor at our being out so late. "The American Colony" must have enjoyed pipes and ale at Price's tap after the performance. Perhaps old Blanchard spun yarns, and Deaf Burk sang like a raven.

Tuesday, 26. Mr. Ducrow having returned, we called on him and made an engagement for two weeks, Levi vaulting one week and riding the second, and myself playing clown to his acts. [He then speaks of mailing letters to C. J. Rogers and Ned Derious:] In the bag of ship Montreal for New York; paid sixpence for the privilege of looking at the New York papers. Rather skinning, that. After tea, went to the Amphitheatre. Ducrow and wife rode a new act, "The Mountain Maid and Tyrolean Shepherd." One of their best; it was a very pretty one. Two children did "The Jingling Jumpers of Pekin." It is the old leaping bar business with the pillars and stump. Dressed Chinese. A new grand pageant in honor of the Queen, using both the ring and the stage. It was magnificent.

"The Mountain Maid, etc" was not new. Ducrow had used it in other seasons, with both Louisa Woolford and his sister, Margaret, as a partner. It appears that the act was got up again especially for the debut of the new bride and groom. Ducrow included a "Musical Burletta Pageant" on the subject of the coronation in June. A few weeks later, an even more ambitious spectacle was mounted, with Mrs. Hillier as the Queen, seated on a richly caparisoned horse atop a platform supported on the shoulders of "her devoted subjects."[92]

Thursday, 28. Now comes the grand day, i.e., the coronation. Cannon commenced firing and bells ringing at half-past three a.m. Everybody traveling. Could not sleep for the uproar, so got up. After breakfast, Cony, Bill, Levi and myself started. The streets were crowded with people in all kinds of vehicles and on foot. After crossing Waterloo Bridge we found difficulty in making headway. We finally worked our way near Charing Cross, where we got a standing place. Such a dense mass of people I never saw before---thousands on thousands, as many as the streets could hold; and the housetops crowded; also the whole fronts of the houses, where galleries had been erected, and single seats sold for from one to five guineas. The way was cleared by the police and mounted Life Guard. The procession came in sight--- first the band and mounted household troops, and the Ambassadors Extraordinary in splendid coaches. The most beautiful was that of Marshal Soult, who was cheered by the multitude enthusiastically. Next came the different ministers, whose coaches were very gorgeous; with the exception of the American minister's, which was very plain. Next came the royal family, Duke of Sussex, Prince George of Cambridge and staff officers, Duke of Wellington, Lord Hill and Her Majesty's household in twelve splendid coaches, each drawn by six horses. Last was the state coach containing Queen Victoria, a magnificent affair drawn by eight creams. It appeared as if built entirely of gold. When she passed the air rang with shouts which made the ground shake. The procession was about an hour in passing; and I never expect to see such a beautiful sight again.

Victoria had become Queen of England on June 20, 1837, following the death of her uncle, King William IV. Coronation Day, which took place on June 28, 1838, began badly, with a cold shower around 8:00 a.m., but soon cleared off. The procession started from Buckingham Palace at 10:00 a.m. and reached Westminster Abbey at 11:30. There the ceremony proceeded smoothly until 3:45, after which the Queen entertained a dinner party of one hundred guests and, in the evening, witnessed the fireworks discharged in Green Park.

We elbowed our way out of the crowd after some difficulty and started for Hyde Park to visit the fair, which was the largest ever in England--- something like six hundred booths of all descriptions, shows, taverns, and gingerbread shops. And all kinds of sports were going on---swings, roundabouts, target shooting, donkey riding, etc. Went into Clarke's Circus; got something to eat; and got home at five o'clock, heartily tired. After tea, went to Victoria Theatre. Waited until Cony and Bill had done playing. At ten, started for a walk to see the illuminations. The streets were crowded as they were during the day. The houses were splendidly illuminated with gas, variegated lamps, etc., with all kinds of devices. The club houses were the most magnificent, being entirely covered with lights having the appearance of temples of gaslight. We made our way to Hyde Park, the fair still going on with the same vigor, and more people than during the day. A grand display of fireworks took place, this beyond description. We left at three a.m., the shows still open, having exhibited in the morning. Old Clarke said he had given thirty-two exhibitions. We walked home by daylight.

The fair, comprising an area one-third of Hyde Park, was originally scheduled to last two days, but, due to its success, continued for four. It functioned under a government permit issued to the proprietors of a show that had formerly been under the management of Richardson. The booths were arranged in a rectangle of approximately 1,400 by 1,000 square feet. The one which was said to have attracted the most attention, from its size alone, was that of a Mr. Williams, a celebrated boiled beef monger of the Old Bailey. For a small sum one could sit atop his pavilion to witness the nightly display of fireworks. In other booths, beef, ham, chicken, beer and wine were equally plentiful. Going from food to other matters, one might pass exhibits of fat boys, living skeletons, Irish giants, Welsh dwarfs, two-headed curiosities and other such wonders of nature. There were magicians and tumblers, pony and donkey rides, archery and stick throwing, as well as roundabouts, swings and the like.[93]

Saturday, 30. At ten a.m., went to the Amphitheatre and practiced vaulting, which had been called, Ducrow directing it. It was really amusing to hear him swear at his men, calling them lummoxes, etc. I hardly think a set of Yankees would stand for it.

Ducrow had a quick temper. Charles Dickens gave him the title of "The Napoleon of the Arena." But, for all that, he was said to be exceedingly generous and courageous.

Levi did thirty-one and twenty-seven. Price could not get over twenty-two. Both had boards in the ring, and two parties, English and American.

Monday, (July) 2. At ten a.m. went to the Amphitheatre to rehearse vaulting. Levi did thirty-two. Ducrow swore at his men as usual. After dinner, packed up our dresses for the debut tonight. Half past six, after the first piece, all ready for the trial of skill between the champions of England and America. Levi was frightened almost to death and I sweat like a bull with the excitement. All our friends in front---Cony, Blanchard, Stevens, and their friends. Deaf Burke in the pit, directing the boards how to be fixed. And Yankee Hill, J. Wallack, and Taglioni, the great dancer, also in front, with a great number of foreign ambassadors, nobility, etc. All ready with two boards and two parties, American and English, with flags of two countries posted over the starting place. Price did twenty somersaults. And then came the Yankee and did thirty-three. Then wasn't there shouting! I guess there was. Well satisfied with the result. So much for our debut at the famous Astley's Amphitheatre.

Before Levi and Price go at it again, I will take this opportunity to insert a letter Blackburn sent to his family in Baltimore.[94]

London, July 18, 1838
Dear Parents,
       It is not quite a month since I wrote last, but having an opportunity of sending this by a friend, who leaves here in the *Great Western,* which starts the 21st inst., I

thought I would write to let you know that myself, as well as my friend North, are well and much pleased with our trip. We made our appearance at Astley's Amphitheatre two weeks since in the vaulting—North, as the American champion, vaulting against Mr. Price, the champion of all Europe, having two spring boards in the ring at once, and two parties, American and English, with the colors of each country on the heads of their horses; myself playing clown to the American party. You may well imagine my feelings the first night, as well as North. I must say I was frightened dreadfully; not for myself, but for North. I thought he would be so excited that he might get beat; but the trial came, and such a brilliant audience I never had the honor of making a bow to before; nearly two-thirds ladies; even the four or five front seats in the pit were filled entirely with ladies. Nearly all the foreign ambassadors were in front, also, Taglioni, the great dancer. Great excitement prevailed. When the finish of the vaulting came, the Champion of England (Price) went on to do his row of somersets, and only threw twenty. Then came the applause; they were certain North could not beat it; but the little Yankee went on and beat him scandalously, doing thirty-three. Such a shout I never heard; I thought the house would come down. If I ever felt well, it was just about that time. We have played twelve nights and have been beaten only one. So you see Uncle Sam is ably represented, for we have truly astonished the natives. North rides next week, and they will be more astonished then, for they have no rider to compete with him in this country; and I think I can beat any of them playing clown. I have seen eight clowns already, and none of them are passable. We have not as yet come to any final arrangement with Ducrow for the season, as we only engaged three weeks to show them what we could do. I cannot tell yet whether we shall stop here or not, as we have had letters from two managers—Mr. Cook, at Hull, and Ryan, at Halifax. We shall go where we can do best, for salaries are rather low in this country. Ducrow's best rider only gets £6 pounds per week; and Price, the vaulter, gets the same. A number of other performers get from £1 5s. to £2. He gives North and myself twelve guineas per week.

If we can get a benefit with it, it will do very well. So much for our success; and now I must tell you what I have seen.

Following this, Blackburn writes of the Queen's coronation day, which I'll omit to avoid duplication and pick up with the text following it.

Now for sight No. 2., Monday, July 9th. Went to Hyde park to witness the Grand Review of the Troops by the Queen. After a good deal of trouble, obtained a standing place on a table for two shillings. In all crowds like this, the poor people run with their chairs, to be let for one penny to a crown. More than 200,000 persons were supposed to be on the ground as spectators. The troops were drawing up on a line on our arrival. Shortly afterwards, the Queen arrived in an open carriage. Her attendants followed in three splendid coaches; they, followed by two hundred officers of distinction on horseback, in splendid uniforms. The most conspicuous were Marshal Soult, Duke of Nemours, Lord Wellington, Lord Hill, etc.

After the Queen passed the length of the line, the troops commenced maneuvering; the artillery were fired, also the cavalry, which amounted to about 5,000 men— the Oxford Blues, Life Guard, 10th Hussars, and some others; 3,000 were on jet black horses, the rest bays. This was a noble sight when charging in a body. The infantry firing was splendid—20,000 men firing together and appearing as one crash.

It was over at 3:00 p.m., and I got out of the crowd with some difficulty, well satisfied that this was the best sight I had seen yet. So much for the Grand Review, and now for sight No. 3. July 10th took a wherry to Westminster Bridge, rowed down the Thames and visited the Tower; paid 1s. for admittance, bought a catalogue book, and 1s. for the Beefeater or conductor.

First room, ancient armory, the kings of England and the knights on horseback, with the armor and the identical arms they wore at that time. This was very interesting, something like 30 figures as large as life. Also, different arms used from the time of William the Conqueror to the present day. Next room, Queen Elizabeth's armory, a great number of ancient weapons, instruments of torture—the ax which Charles I, Sir Walter Raleigh, Sally Jane Grey and some others, were beheaded with. Next, the small armory, a room 345 feet in length, containing 270,000 stands of arms. This was a beautiful sight. Walls were embellished with different devices—formed with swords, pistols, bayonets, etc., forming pillars, stars, wreaths, etc. The heavy armory was also very interesting—cannon of every description, from the first made in England to the present day. Also many pieces taken in different battles. Paid 2s. more to see the Crown Jewels. This I could give no idea of, only to think it is a pity they should be there. I should be perfectly satisfied with one diamond from the crown, out of the hundreds it contains. It is worth £112,000, about a half million dollars. We were next shown the room where the Duke of Clarence was drowned in the butt of malmsey, also where Richard III had the princes smothered, besides many other little things quite interesting. On coming home, saw the great Nassau balloon go up with nine persons. This was a grand affair. These are the principal things I have seen since my last.

Joe Blackburn

P.S. The trial of skill between North and Price has drawn the largest houses during the season, and created a great deal of excitement. There is a pretty heavy betting all over the house every night. North got great applause when he done forty-one, and got a medal from Ducrow.

Tuesday, 3. Levi practiced riding; horse did not suit. Told Ducrow that the horse did not suit him, and he was not inclined to lose the good name he had acquired in his own country; that he was as great a man in the United States as Ducrow was in England, and if he rode he must have a horse to suit him. An-

other horse was ordered in, which did very well. Second night Price did twenty-nine, North thirty-one. Hard pushed, he came off victorious. Hurrah for Yankee Doodle and her brood! The English party down in the mouth.

Wednesday, July 4. The glorious anniversary of our independence. Called on Yankee Hill, found him at home, drank two glasses of wine to our home and absent friends, read American papers, looked at American paintings, etc. In vaulting tonight, American party got beat, Price doing thirty-five, the most he had ever done. Hurrahing on their side. Our side had nothing to say.

Thursday, 5. In vaulting, American party again victorious. First, Price twenty-one, Levi twenty-three; Price twenty-six, Levi twenty-nine.

Friday, 6. Levi practiced vaulting and riding; did thirty-five. Price also practiced, tying Levi.

Night vaulting, Price thirty-two, Levi thirty-seven. Now the English party have nothing to brag of. Mr. Ducrow invites us into his private box, which was an unprecedented act with him.

Saturday, 7. Vaulting again. Astonished the natives. Price did twenty-six, Levi thirty-nine. Price tried again; did twenty-one. Levi just topped him, doing twenty-three. The house fairly shook again with shouts.

Monday, 9. The vaulting record: Levi thirty-five, Price thirty.

Tuesday, 10. Levi thirty-four, Price thirty.

Wednesday, 11. Levi thirty-nine, Price twenty-nine.

Thursday, 12. Levi thirty-six and thirty-two; Price thirty and twenty-three.

Friday, 13. Price thirty-two; Levi forty-one. Immense applause from the audience. First time forty somersaults has been done in England.

Saturday, 14. Price thirty-five; Levi thirty-six. A close contest and great excitement among the audience. Saw bills for next week; found Levi in for horsemanship and vaulting. Did not agree to do but one. Wrote note to Ducrow to that effect. Stopped in the Amphitheatre till twelve in hopes of getting an answer.

Sunday, 15. Ten a.m. Our note was returned by Ducrow's servant, Arthur, stating that it could not be received until it came in a proper manner---that is, sealed. A few minutes after, Mr. Ducrow's factotum, Broadfoot, called and excused the matter of putting Levi in for two acts, and wished to know what our intentions were in shape of an engagement. We deferred answering him until next week.

Monday, 16. At night Levi road very well. Vaulting, Levi thirty-five, Price thirty-two.

Tuesday, 17. North thirty-four, Price twenty-three.

Wednesday, 18. Levi thirty-five, Price thirty.

Thursday, 19. Levi gave them a big pile--- forty-four; Price thirty-two. After the performance, took a stroll to see some of the life in London. First place stopped at was the Shades, about three stories underground. Here there was singing and drinking going on.

Friday, 20. Levi thirty-seven, Price twenty-nine.

Saturday, 21. Levi thirty-one, Price thirty-three, being the second time Levi has been beaten in three weeks. Had some words with Broadfoot about engagement.

Sunday, 22. Had a note from Mr. Ducrow that he had taken us out of next week's bill. This was a finale to our playing at Astley's.

Monday, 23. At night went in front at Astley's. On coming out, was told by doorkeeper that Mr. West was insulted by our not coming to terms, and our further admission was stopped. Did not care a damn.

Tuesday, 24. Eight p.m., went to Haymarket Theatre; saw three pieces---an olio by Messrs. Seguin, Frazer, Mrs. Waylett and Mrs. Honey, finishing with "New Notions," in which my old friend Yankee Hill appeared and caused much laughter.

These actors were serio-comic singing artists. Edward Seguin, a basso, was a graduate of the British Academy of Music. After making his theatrical debut in 1831, he became known as the superior to any in his field. Frazer was a tenor of some importance, who, like Seguin, was soon to perform in America. Mrs. Waylett was called "one of the most charming singers and piquant actresses of the century;" and Mrs. Honey "could always draw delighted audiences by her singing and acting." The two were praised for "beauty of voice, exquisite method and expression."[95]

Thursday, 26. Received a letter from Ryan, giving us our terms. After dinner wrote a long letter to Ducrow, giving a full explanation of Broadfoot's conduct.

Friday, 27. In the afternoon, Levi had an interview with Ducrow, who was sorry that any misun-

*derstanding had happened, and said his house was
always open to us for any time and any length of time.*

*Saturday 28. Went to the Italian Opera with
Ducrow; drank champagne, ate ice cream, and ogled
the ladies through a double-barreled spyglass.*

*Tuesday, 31. On arriving at the steamer, met
Deaf Burke, who came to see us off to Yorkshire to
join Ryan's company. Passed down "Old Father
Thames," as they call it, but it is not much larger
than a good sized creek in America. Passage to Hull
was to be ten shillings, but they generally manage to
make it up to double by their genteel way of robbery.
For instance: dinner, 2s. 6d.; bed, 2s. 6d.; steward's
fee, 1s. 6d.; supper, bread and butter and bad tea,
2s.; breakfast, worse coffee and bread, 2s. This is not
highway robbery, but piracy in a small way. Got to
bed at eleven p.m---that is, if you could call it a bed,
one foot by five. I managed to lay in it edgewise for
the night.*

Blackburn is off to join Ryan's company in the
north central area of England. At this time we are
seeing the beginning of the era of great urban growth,
a growth so rapid that by 1851 more than half the
population were living in municipalities of 10,000 or
more. Chiefly, this occurred because of a migration
from rural areas to accommodate the need for a non-
seasonal work force. The Manchester-Salford region
quadrupled in size during this period. The industrial
centers of Liverpool, Birmingham, Leeds, and Sheffield showed similar population increases. Ryan was
well aware of this changing demographic and conducted his routing to take full advantage of it. His ter-

ritory encompassed these major cities and the surrounding industrial communities.

>*Monday, August 1. [They arrived at Hull, where they saw old Cooke and James Cooke, who were building a circus. Further details of their journey are uninteresting to the general reader until he chronicles their arrival at Leeds.]*
>
>*So here I am at my birthplace. Passed up Kirkgate. Saw the sign of the Golden Cock, next door to which I was born. What a change! Twenty-five years ago I was running over this ground in petticoats. Now I am strutting over it with high-heeled boots and a pearl handled cane.*
>
>*Arrived at Halifax at seven p.m. After supper went to the circus and reported to Ryan, the manager, a thick-set man, who squints, but appears to be clever. Witnessed the performances, which were good and of quite a variety, a Mr. Powell being the best rider---tolerable.[96] Finished with a pantomime in which the celebrated Dick Usher played Clown very good.[97]*

Our travelers had sailed up the Suffock and Norfolk coastline, through the waters of the North Sea, into the mouth of the Humber River, which formed an inlet bay at Hull. They then traveled on to Leeds, some fifty or sixty miles west along the Aire River, an off-shoot of the Humber. From Leeds, Halifax was a short distance to the south and west.

James Ryan (1799-1875) was proprietor of one of the best circuses in England for many years. Throughout his career he erected amphitheatres in Bristol, Sheffield, and Birmingham, the latter city be-

ing his stronghold. He eventually went broke there in
an attempt to create a new, brick building for his circus performances. As a manager, he had a reputation
of being kind to his employees. Credited as one of the
cleverest tightrope dancers in the world, he was also
an accomplished rider, and tumbler. Ryan's squinting
was caused by his having only one eye.[98] There were
several Powells in the circus business but the one
mentioned above has to be William MacDonnell Powell (1816-1900) who had been performing with
Batty's company in Liverpool, Newcastle, Nottingham, and Cork. While a principal equestrian with
Ryan in 1837, he married into the Hengler circus
family. At this time he was billed as the "First Rider
of the Age."[99] Richard "Dicky" Usher was a native of
Liverpool and a popular entertainer there at the
Olympic Circus from as early as 1808. A trainer of
geese and cats, he was the first clown to use the trick
of being pulled down river in a tub by a pair of
geese.[100]

*Friday, (Aug.) 3. Levi practiced vaulting. Did
thirty-four, rather astonishing them, being the most
they had ever seen.*

*Saturday, 4. Levi practiced. Did thirty-seven,
which astonished them still more.*

*Monday, 6. [Blackburn and North made their
first appearance in Ryan's company, and the historian
writes:] Levi did thirty-six. Had a fine horse and he
received great applause.*

[This ends Log No. 6. Log. No. 7 begins.]

*Wednesday, August 8. Had a good house, the
parson of the parish and family being a part of the
audience. One thing I forgot to mention, which I have*

notice in all companies: the box officers and door-keepers in Ryan's establishment are women, composed of the manager's wife and the wives of the performers. Nearly all the performers are married. There are no less than fifty-two children living, belonging to members of this company. It is invariably the same with theatricals and equestrians. Each will have a wife to support on small salaries, which generally vary from one to two pounds per week.

Friday, 10. Old Dick Usher's benefit, very full house. Pleased with one of his gags, being drawn in a carriage by four real cats. It was very funny.

Monday, 13. [David, the colored man referred to as living at Cony's in London, was now keeping house for Blackburn and North.] Negroes are a great curiosity in Yorkshire. Our boy David went out to see a party of gypsies out of town. On his arrival at their encampment, other persons of the same view turned to looking at him, he being the greater curiosity; which so annoyed him that he shortly bent his steps homeward, the whole crowd following, many of whom took him to be North, the great American vaulter, as most of the people here think all Americans are black. At the circus, Mr. Ryan did a new scene on three horses, called "The Woodcutter," which was truly wonderful.[101]

Wednesday, 15. Arranged with Ryan to remain six months. Night at circus, a beautiful entry done, called "The Captive Bride."

Friday, 17. Two letters from America, one from Sam Phillips and one from Charley Rogers. Read them over two or three times before the performance.

Sunday, 19. David learning to sing "Jim Crow," to sing at Rivers' benefit, Thursday next. He is announced as the real American (Niggers are getting ripe.).

Sam Phillips was ringmaster with Brown's circus, 1834-36, and was a member of the 1838 Bacon & Derious company. Charley Rogers, of course, was the Charles J. Rogers of Spalding & Rogers fame.

Dick Rivers was the patriarch of a circus family of riders, tumblers and posturers, whose performing sons included Frank, Charles, Richard, Luke and Frederick, all of whom became prominent in the American arenas.

See by London and Leeds papers that my friend John Reilly of Cincinnati has had twenty-four chickens hatched by one hen. This is a long way for such news to come---nearly four thousand miles.

Wednesday, 22. Rivers parading the streets with a large stone he is to break on his breast tonight for his benefit. What gags! And the people stand it. Measured for a suit of clothes; did not like buttons with a crown on them---too democratic. North did forty; received six rounds of applause. The big stone got hissed. Daves "Jim Crow" was a perfect failure.

Thursday, 23. Made our bill for North's benefit; put him in vaulting clogs. Received a letter from Ben Stickney, which he speaks of the arrival of VanAmburgh in London, also that Price had done forty in practice and thirty-nine in public.

VanAmburgh sailed for London on the *Pennsylvania*, leaving New York City, July 7, 1838. He first appeared at Astley's Amphitheatre, and later at Drury Lane and the principal cities of Europe. In January of 1839, the Queen visited the Drury Lane Theatre to witness VanAmburgh's performance. It so pleased her that she commissioned Sir Edwin Landseer to paint a picture of him with his lions, which was put on exhibition that same year.[102] While abroad, dramas were written for him and were produced with success. He made several tours through the provinces of England, Ireland, Scotland and Wales with a traveling menagerie, introducing the American style of tenting to Great Britain. In 1845, after seven years overseas, he returned to the United States.

VanAmburgh was at Astley's Amphitheatre shortly after he first arrived in England. *Bell's Life in London* of August 26, 1838, carried a description of a performance with his cats which reveals the state of wild beast taming at that time. Two immense wooden cages were placed on the stage. Young VanAmburgh, dressed in a plain white jacket, entered one of them in which were a lion, a lioness, a Bengal tiger, and tree leopards. He proceeded to fondle the animals in a show of friendship between man and beast. Going a few steps further, he pried open the mouth of the lion with his hands, made him present his paw and ended by riding on the animal's back. He was equally familiar with the lioness and the tiger. The leopards were more exuberant. They jumped around and upon him in a playful manner, one alighting on his head and shoulders, and others leaping over his arm as he extended it outward. He gave commands by a motion of his fingers and teased them with a small whip. They seemed in perfect subjection, offering no resistance. He next entered the second cage, in which there was another lion, lioness and two leopards. This lion showed great fear by sidling into a corner and remaining there until he was driven out by means of a whip. Just as in the first cage, the other animals were commanded to jump on and about him; after which, the lion was placed in a prone position while VanAmburgh reposed on his shaggy mane. This was followed by the tamer placing his head in the animal's mouth. Finally, for what seems to have been the closing effect, VanAmburgh brought a lamb into the cage; the cats showed not the slightest disposition to attack the woolly creature. With this bit of biblical enactment, the entire display of the mastery of man over beasts was successfully concluded.

Thursday, 30. Heavy thunder storm, of course, being our benefit. Had thirty-four pounds, two shillings, a good house for the fag end of the season. North rode his principal and Indian act, which pleased well. Also did twenty somersaults in clogs, thirty-six without. I played clown to his acts with great success.

[Our friends' next journey was a flying trip by coach and rail to Liverpool; where, it is recorded, they:] Called on Jim Ward, the boxer; also Phil Sampson, noted in the prize ring.[103]

[The next day they:] Called on Langham, the boxer who fought Spring.

It was usual at this time of undeveloped railroad systems for the traveler to share the facilities of both stage and rail to arrived at a given destination. Blackburn probably used the Liverpool and Manchester Railway. This line was opened for the first time on September 15, 1830. By 1836 it was carrying 450,000 passengers a year. Although there was great progress in rail development, none of the lines in the country were fully completed.

In addition to rail building, advancement in motive power was being achieved. For example, the *North Star*, a locomotive constructed for the Great Western Railway Company, was said to run fifty miles an hour when pulling a fifty ton cargo (eighty with only the tender attached).

Tom Spring's real name was Winter. It was said that he changed his name to conform to his mild and cheerful disposition. Not a slugger, he won his bouts through his sparring ability. He was designated champion on the retirement of Tom Cribb; after which, he was challenged by the Irish champion, John Langham. Spring, at 190 pounds, defeated Langham, 176 pounds, for the English heavyweight title in 1824. The fight took place in a turf ring at the Worcester race course, where more than thirty thousand spectators were in attendance. After seventy-seven rounds, two hours and twenty-nine minutes, Langham failed to get up in the allotted time, giving Spring the victory. A rematch was scheduled. This time the fight was more evenly conducted, with the advantage shifting back and forth for seventy-six rounds, until Langham was forced to give in. Spring retired after this win, opened an inn, and continued to prosper. Langham's popularity with his Irish followers was so great that even in defeat he was acclaimed.[104]

[Log No. 8 begins.]

Monday, September 3. Went to Jim Wards. Saw Bell's Life and found that Price had challenged North to vault for one hundred pounds.

Price's letter was published in the *Bell's Life in London* of September 2: [105]

VAULTING CHALLENGE.
TO THE EDITOR OF BELL'S LIFE IN LONDON.

Sir—Observing in a provincial newspaper (Halifax) a challenge from Mr. North, late of Astley's Theatre, to any person in the world, to throw the greatest number of somersets for £5,000, I have only to say, that, unless that gentleman has turned potato merchant, and means 500 lbs., the sum is too great for myself to raise, and I may also presume for him too; but if £100 are in his eyes worth contending for, I will myself compete with him for the last named sum, to throw the greatest number of somersets for six successive nights (or days), to have three attempts each night or day, as may be hereafter agreed, the person throwing the greatest number of somersets at the end of the week to be declared the winner. Should so humble an individual as myself, and the sum I have named be worthy his attention, I am ready at a day's notice to contend with him; the conditions of the wager can be settled between us, and if Mr. North chooses to come to London to decide it I will pay half his expenses. To show I am in earnest, £25 of my money I have deposited in the hands of our worthy treasurer, Mr. Foster, and the rest is forthcoming at any time or place.

I remain, Sir, your obedient servant,

Thomas Price

Vaulter at Astley's Theatre, Aug. 31, 1838

[They rejoined Ryan's company in Ashton in time for the night's performance.][106]

Tuesday, 4. Answered Price's challenge. Thursday, 6. Little Dick Rivers, practicing, put his elbow out.

Tuesday, 11. Received lots of news from America; letters from Sam Phillips, John Gossin and Alex Downie. Also received a Baltimore paper, with one of my letters published. I little thought that the climate of England would make me a literary man.

Wednesday, 12. A small package arrived; supposed to be a large playbill and some papers sent by Alex Downie. Did not take it in. Postage too high--- only three pounds, 3s. 2d., about fifteen dollars. North, vaulting, did forty-five. This is the fourth time he has done this number, twice in America and twice in England.

Thursday, 13. A very full house on account of being patronized by the Earl of Stamford. Get the bigwigs to come in this country and you are sure of a big house.

Friday, 14. Received letter from Ben Stickney. Says Price is backing out. Charley Rivers did two somersaults first time.[107]

Tuesday, 18. Levi received letter from Price, saying that he could not stick to his last Sunday's challenge in Bell's Life, hoping Levi would not notice it. I answered it, but did not answer his letter.

Monday, 24. Went to Duckfield Wakes, which is their annual feast, a fair on a small scale.

Wakes, which assumed the identity of fairs, originated from the annual celebrations of the church's consecration or from the feast day of the saint in whose name the church was dedicated. Gradually, the religious aspect of the festivals diminished, replaced by more secular events, affording hard working men and women an opportunity to vent their need for merry-making and revelry.[108]

There were two shows. Visited the theatre, which had over the front, "Williamson's Pantomimic and Dramatic Theatre." Paid one penny a piece, and was ushered into this temple of the Muses. We saw a tragedy in two acts---only three persons to play it, comic song, and pantomime. All finished in ten minutes. We were shown out the back door. And fun commenced again outside: clown told a story, the heavy-tragedy man was beating the bass drum, while Lady Macbeth was dancing a straight four with three others. Close beside the theatre was another exhibition of less pretensions; it was the painting of some murder, as natural as life. All to be seen for one halfpenny. They also had their outside parade: an old woman showed some tricks of sleight-of-hand, such as the egg bag, and a little boy sang "All 'Round My Hat," accompanied by an old man on the pandean pipes and bass drum.

Tuesday, (Oct.) 2. Played under the patronage of Lord Wilton, who did not come. Good house.

Wednesday, 3. Parrish's company of theatricals arrived.

Thursday, 4. The actors erecting their booth next to our circus.

Friday, 5. The actors, playing for threepence only for admission, had about one pound in. Played "Dumb Wife of Manchester" and "Sudden Thoughts." Playing better than any concern of the kind I have yet seen. The establishment, inside and out, very neat, and larger than Richardson's famous booth.

Saturday, 6. Saw a funny dance at the theatre by two persons dressed as soldiers in front and sailors behind, with masks on the back of their heads. After dancing a while as soldiers, they turn and finish with a hornpipe. This had a good effect.

Monday, 22. North did forty-six, the most he has ever done before an audience.

Tuesday, 23. During the performance we were astonished by the appearance in front of Price, the vaulter, accompanied by Hughes, the rider. Levi and myself met them after the performance at the Ashton and spent an agreeable evening.

Wednesday, 24. At eleven a.m., met Price again. Said he had come to make the match. Levi told him that all he had to do was to back up his money. This he would not accede to without making new arrangements. Levi said he could have nothing to do with him except in the way agreed on in Bell's Life. So Price backed entirely out of all he had stated through that paper, and Levi left him. He got very wrathy after Levi left, saying that he had not backed out and that he could beat any damned Yankee that could ever come over the Atlantic. I told him that I intended to bring two or three little boys next summer from America that would leave him far behind. Wasn't he mad? Threatened to pull my long nose; but that was after I left. He cleared out about three p.m., disgusted with himself and everyone else.

Sunday, (Nov.) 4. Dropped in at the Commercial---fat landlord, fat brother, fat mother, fat sister, two uncomfortably fat dogs, and a fat cat. Took two glasses of ale and leaned for home. At three p.m. bade farewell to the good town of Ashton and took passage for Manchester. Put up at the Concert Tavern, next door to the Queen's Theatre, kept by one Thompson---a clever fellow and keeps a good house. The evening was spent very comfortably in Thomp-

son's parlor. Among the company was Tom Oliver, a man of much notoriety in the prize ring, a fine looking old chap with whiskers silver-white.

Tom Oliver was one of the long list of pugilists defeated by Spring. In an earlier fight with Ned Painter in 1814, which lasted only four minutes and a half, Oliver was the victor. English boxing writer, Pierce Egan, described the fray with these colorful words:[109]

> Such a complete determined milling round is not to be met with in the Annals of Pugilism, and there was more execution done in it than in many fights of an hour's length. It was enough to finish any two men.... They were both punished in the extreme, and Painter was quite blind, and his nose beat flat upon his face. Oliver's body was terribly beaten, his head much disfigured, and one of his eyes nearly closed.

[They took coach for Bradford the next morning, where they opened "to a crowded house."][110]

Thursday, 8. [He jumped on the Leeds coach and visited that city. A fair was going on, and Wombwell's Menagerie was on exhibition. Of the latter he writes:] Went into Wombwell's wild beast show. A very good collection, but I have seen better. They are not what Englishmen represent them to be in America. The elephant wagon is the greatest curiosity, containing three elephants---one tolerable-sized one, and two small ones. The wagon is twenty-two feet long, ten feet wide, and eighteen in height. Runs on six wheels, each seventeen inches wide. All the cages were large, the band good, but the men were the worse lot of loafers I have seen attached to any exhibition. The admission was one shilling. Went into another smaller exhibition of animals for one penny. t had about eight cages.

George Wombwell (1777-1850) was the first great traveling menagerie proprietor. His entry into the menagerie business began in 1805 with the purchase of a pair of huge boa constrictors. With them he organized a caravan and began his tours of England. In 1825 Wombwell stirred up public indignation, not to mention vigorous publicity for his establishment, by baiting two lions, one at a time, with several large dogs. One of the lions was so tame that he merely fended the canine aggressors off. The other, a more savage animal, quickly maimed them so ferociously they had to be dragged through the bars of the cage.[111]

Monday, 12. Arrived at Sheffield.[112] [The next day he received a visit from his uncle John.] A fine old man of sixty-seven, in knee breeches and gaiters; much pleased to see me; drinks gin and keeps cows. [Mr. Blackburn seems to have taken a vacation, for on the 4th he:] Took a coach for Leeds. In the evening visited the theatre, next door to the Elephant and Castle. Saw "The Merchant of Venice." Mr. Creswick as Shylock tolerable.

William Creswick (b. 1813) made his debut in 1831. Shortly thereafter, he emigrated to America and successfully performed in both the United States and Canada. He then returned to England and was well received by the English audiences. According to Ireland, his acting was "marked by great earnestness and entire regardlessness of the traditions and conventionalities of the profession."[113] Eventually, he became the manager of the Surrey Theatre, London.

Monday, 19. [He appeared with Ryan.]

Saturday, December 1. Batty, the manager, in front. Levi gave him forty-four somersaults. Met him after the performance. He looks a good deal like my old manager, Ben Brown;[114] but he does not possess half so much good sense, having too much low black-guardism in his composition.

Sunday, 2. Goose for dinner. Just as we had commenced operating on it, who should drop in but our old friends Cony and Blanchard; who had come from Wakefield where they open tomorrow.

Saturday, 8. Shows of all description begin to flock into town. Batty's wild beast show commenced operations by the side of our place.

Sunday, 9. Ten a.m., took a gig and drove out to Wakefield to see Cony and Blanchard. Spent a very pleasant day with them. Left for home at four p.m. Had not got more than six miles on our journey before we struck a pile of stones. Horses and gig upset in the ditch, Levi standing on his head in the mud, I walking on my hands in the road, surrounded by yokels.

Tuesday, 11. Got letter from Cooke at Nottingham in relation to a letter published in Baltimore concerning him. Answered it.

In a letter to a friend in Cincinnati, Blackburn had written that old Cooke was bitter about Americans, claiming they had burned him out in Baltimore out of jealousy, and that they had also tried to burn

his property twice afterwards.[115] Cooke seems to have
heard about Blackburn's correspondence.

*[The record of the week ending Saturday, 16,
is:]*[116] *Thin business on account of the opposition of
Wombwell's show.*

*Monday, December 17. The following list of
Wombwell's show was given me by Sam Berry:
George Wombwell, proprietor; eleven carriages containing beasts, one carriage or house for family, one
stage or platform wagon, one band wagon, forty-four
horses, thirty men, one hundred and eighty animals;
large carriage containing elephants, weighing up-
wards of seventeen tons, drawn by twelve horses.*

*Thursday, 20. North's benefit; rode six horses
for the first time, well; vaulting thirty-seven, and in
clogs eighteen; all to a damned bad house of nineteen
pounds.*

*[Blackburn again visits Leeds and mentions
particularly the children of a relative knocking at his
door on a Christmas morning and singing: "I wish
you a merry Christmas, happy New Year, pockets full
of money, belly full of cheer." He rejoined North on
December 26th and reappeared.] Thursday, 27. Went
with Dick Rivers as far as savings bank, where he deposited twenty pounds, a wonderful thing for an actor
to do.*

*Saturday, 29. Only tolerable business at night,
this being only an experimental night---Ryan never
being in the habit of performing on Saturday night
before in this place. People here prefer drinking, etc.,
on this night.*

*Monday, 31. Randal treated me the first time!
Make a long chalk.*

Tuesday, (Jan.) 15. North received a Glengary cup from Batty.

Saturday, 26. Dinner given to part of the company at Greggs', Hammer Lane. Champion of the lightweights was there, a very civil young man, twenty-two years of age. Has won eighteen fights.

Thursday, 31. Patronized by Prince Louis Napoleon Bonaparte. Good house. The prince, a good looking young man of about thirty, with mustache. North did thirty-nine, the prince applauding greatly both his vaulting and his riding.

Friday, February 1. North met with an adventure this morning. In returning from an excursion in the country, his carriage was stopped by a man, the door was opened, and his cane was seized. In his attempt to wrest it from Levi's hands, the naked sword came out; upon the sight of which the cove decamped.

Monday, 4. Harper, the Negro singer arrived to commence an engagement of one week. Was very successful the first night. Sings well. Levi did his new scene, "The Morning and Evening Star."

Sunday, 10. My birthday, twenty-nine years old.

Tuesday, 12. Six o'clock a.m., took post chaise for the purpose of seeing the fight between Burke and Bendigo. Passed through Yarmouth sixteen miles. Went eight miles to Appleby House. Here found many people congregated. Followed the crowd to the scene of action, to the right of Appleby House about six miles. There were thousands of people on the grounds previous to our arrival, which was at one o'clock p.m. The ring was already formed. After a tedious wait, the fight com-menced at two p.m. and lasted only twenty-four minutes. It terminated in favor of Bendigo after eleven rounds, Burke butting in the last, which was against the new rules. Neither of the men hurt. Got home, after traveling sixty miles to see a bad fight.

"Deaf" Burke returned to England in 1838. That year the Broughton's Rules, which had been in use for nearly one hundred years, was replaced with the London Prize Ring Rules. The Burke/Bendigo contest was the first to be conducted under these new guidelines. After winning this fight with Burke, Bendigo, whose real name was William Thompson, suffered an injury to his knee and was forced to retire from the ring. On losing, Burke passed into oblivion, except for the attention of Joe Blackburn.[117]

[Blackburn has now "laid off" for several days on account of a cold.]
Friday, 22. I went to the theatre. Mrs. Honey sang "Zurich's Waters" and "Beautiful Rhine" charmingly, better than I ever heard before.
Sunday, (Mar.) 3. Received letter from Charles J. Rogers, Cincinnati. One month coming.
Monday 11. Received news of Price doing fifty somersaults at Glasgow. At night North did forty-eight, most he has done yet before an audience.
Saturday, 16. Went to theatre. Saw young Pablo Fanque on the tight rope, attended by his daddy, a Negro.

William Darby (1796-1871) was an equestrian, acrobat, and rope-walker, who later became a circus proprietor. After being orphaned at an early age, he became apprenticed to William Batty. His early billing was as "Young Darby," but he adopted the name "Pablo Fanque" sometime in the 1830s. He went into management in 1841 and continued until his death.[118]

> *Wednesday, 20. North did fifty.*
>
> *Friday, 29. This being Good Friday, no play at the circus. A public dinner was given to Levi at the Warwick Arms for the purpose of presenting him with a medal; which was done by old Dick Rivers, the stage manager, in the presence of fifty gentlemen, mostly the citizens of Birmingham. Rivers made a very appropriate speech, which was answered by Levi. The medal is a beautiful one costing twenty pounds.*
>
> *Saturday, 30. End of the engagement with Ryan. Hicken, the first English horseman, refused to subscribe to North's medal. O Crickey!*
>
> *Monday, April 1. Opened in the Amphitheatre, Liverpool, under the management of Bates.*

Bates must have been managing for Batty. While with Batty's circus in Henley, North accomplished his greatest feat when he became the first rider to turn a somersault while on the back of a running horse. He repeated the feat in the United States at the Bowery Theatre in 1840 while with Welch & Bartlett's Circus.

> *Monday, 15. Visited the Theatre Royal. Heard Braham sing "The Death of Nelson," "A Man's a Man for a' That," and some others. Don't think much of him.*

The performer at the Theatre Royal was probably John Braham, the most renowned of English vocalists. He had made large sums of money and lived in princely style, but bad speculation in 1835 severely reduced his savings. At this time, 1839, he was sixty-seven years old; but, indeed, he still performed into his eighties. Of his appearance at the Park Theatre, New York City, in 1840, Ireland observed, "As an actor, he was tame and insipid, and his age and diminutive appearance (being only five feet three inches in height) were serious drawbacks on his powers of attraction...."[119] Chalk up another one for Blackburn. It is possible, however, that the singer was Braham's son, Augustus, who was performing at this time as well.

Friday, 19. VanAmburgh called to see me. He opens at the Theatre Royal next week. Mr. Smith came with him. He is connected with the business.

[On Monday, 22, Blackburn, Ben Stickney and wife and child sailed for America on board the Hibernia, Captain Cobb. Prior to his departure from Liverpool, the entries in the diary indicate failing health; and he writes in one instance:] Put a plaster on my chest; this climate does not agree with me.

[The last entry is at sea; but evidently he is not in his usual spirits, for the diary of the homeward voyage lacks the humor of the outward sail. It chronicles but few events---two or three rows in the steerage, and a mention of assisting Captain Cobb in the preparation of a code of rules for the government of the steerage passengers. A letter from Blackburn in Baltimore to North in Liverpool, under the date of Baltimore, July 3, Blackburn writes his "Dear Levi"

*in excellent spirits. He speaks of having arrived in
New York after a pleasant voyage of thirty days. Alas!
Dave, the colored man, and quite likely the first of his
race who ever appeared in minstrel song and dance in
England, on his return to America, fell from grace.]
"I left Dave in New York and did not see him after
landing, although I remained one week. He brought
my trunk up to Tom Grundy's, and that was the last I
saw of him. When I looked in my trunk, I found myself
minus all my shirts except three. I lay that to his English education. * * * Believe me, there is no place like
home. Remember me to all the folks that side of the
pond that I know, except Price. He is the only man I
hate in the world, and him I thoroughly hate." [After
gossip about mutual acquaintances all over the country, he concludes with a fervent, "God bless you!"]*

The circus, as part of an American entertainment industry, had reached a maturity by the time Joe Blackburn returned from England in the spring of 1840. The techniques of moving from place to place, setting up the tented arena, and taking it down and loading for transport elsewhere had become standard. The acts within the circus program were the same from one troupe to the next. The methods of advertising were identical. Although many artists were imported from England and the Continent, there was an increasing number indigenous to this side of the Atlantic of equal virtuosity and versatility. The genre had developed within a period of democratic nationalism to become "American bred"; unlike theatrical performance and operation, which was adopted almost wholesale from England. Perhaps the only real foreign similarity was a reliance on equestrianism. Most performers could find year-around employment by touring the country towns in the summer and working within permanent or semi-permanent city amphitheatres during the winter season. At this point in the century, if one may personify, the circus could look to a long and healthy life.

Fire, the dreaded nemesis of nineteenth century theatre owners and an unwanted burden on the already tenuous financial operation of theatricals, appears to have followed in the wake of the travelers within our diary. The Mobile theatre was burned to the ground in the early morning hours of November

20, 1838. Supposedly, the cause was from fireworks used in the blowing up of a mill in the performance of "The Miller and His Men," (a melodrama by Isaac Pocock) the previous night. Ludlow, who was the lessee, was uninsured. He lost his entire stock of scenery, wardrobe, music and books. The Charleston Theatre was razed on April 27, 1838, a month following Blackburn's departure from that city. Starting in some out-building on the corner of King and Beresford Streets, the flames spread from one structure to another, destroying the market, the Universalist Church, the theatre, and nearly a thousand houses, with great loss of life. New York's National Theatre burned on the afternoon of September 23, 1839, the work of an arsonist. The owners were partially insured, but James Wallack, the lessee, lost all his stage properties and theatrical paraphernalia. The Bowery Theatre, which had burned on February 18, 1838, was again demolished on April 25, 1845. The fire originated in the carpenter shop, spread to the gas house, and finally to the theatre. Nothing was saved.

The bursting of a camphene lamp set the old National Theatre in Washington ablaze on the evening of March 5, 1845. The conflagration started in an out-building where lamps were trimmed during a performance of the fairy burletta, "Beauty and the Beast." The theatre was cleared in an orderly fashion, with no injury or loss of life.

What became of the English managers with whom Blackburn and North were connected? On June 8, 1841, Astley's Theatre was destroyed by fire, creating a loss of £20,000. This was a severe blow to Ducrow, who collapsed under the strain. Weakened in body and mind, he died on January 27, 1842. After the fire, William Batty brought his company to London and opened at the converted National Baths, in Westminster Bridge Road. He took over the lease on the new Astley's Amphitheatre in 1843, after the break-up of Ducrow's troupe, but, as fortune would have it, the building burned down again. While another structure was being designed and built, he returned to the National Baths, where he opened Batty's Equestrian Arena. Astley's New Royal Amphitheatre of Arts opened later in 1843, which became the home for Batty's circus until 1853. Batty died on February 7, 1868; after which, Astley's was sold to Sanger.[120]

James Ryan had erected amphitheatres in Birmingham, Sheffield, Bristol, and other towns, but the construction of a new brick building in Birmingham in 1841 was his downfall. It failed the following year. He continued touring for a while but in 1848 his company was taken over by the bailiffs. Ryan then worked for other proprietors, but in later years became eccentric. He died in Paris in poverty in 1875.[121]

It has been stated that, once back in America, Blackburn took to the stage and became a capable low comedian. I have not been able to confirm this. For the next few years, however, he was occupied as equestrian director with the Philadelphia Circus (James Raymond and Noell E. Waring, proprietors) in 1840; equestrian director at the Bowery Amphitheatre, New York City, on April 5, 1841, for a bill made up of featured equestrian stars. He joined the western unit of June, Titus, Angevine & Co. for the tenting season of that year; but in November, was back in New Orleans where arenic performances were being staged at the St. Charles Theatre by manager

Caldwell. Quite likely there was a reunion with his friend North at that time, for North appeared there under a week's contract in mid-December.

Health seems to have been a continuing plague since Blackburn returned to America. Left a "fortune" by a deceased uncle, he was on his way from New Orleans to Baltimore to claim it, when he became sick and died on the Mississippi steamboat, *Express Mail*, near Horse Shoe Bend. His body was laid to rest in Memphis. Thus ended the career of "Gentleman Joe," clown and author of these logs. The following item from a Memphis newspaper explains the funeral rite at his grave:[122]

> The respective companies met according to previous notice, for the purpose of paying that respect due to the worth and talents of the late Joseph Blackburn. The procession then formed in front of the Commercial Hotel, Messrs. Garson and Claveau taking the lead. Then followed the New Orleans band, drawn in a car by six horses, followed by the New York band, drawn by six horses. The rear was brought up by the performers, citizens, etc., on horseback, bearing the usual badge of mourning on the left arm. The procession then proceeded to the burial ground, where it formed in a circle around the grave of the deceased: the bands played a dirge suited to the occasion; each member took the badge from his arm and placed it as a tribute of respect upon the grave of their departed friend. Mr. Garson and Mr. Herbert made neat and appropriate addresses on the occasion, after which the procession returned to the city.

North had returned to the United States in the fall of 1840. In January of 1841 he opened a sixteen week engagement with Welch, Bartlett & Co. at the Bowery Theatre under the management of Thomas Hamblin; during which time his trophies from the tour of England, the gold medal from Ryan's company and a silver and gold snuff box from Batty's, were put on display at the Branch Coffee House, a resort of actors and equestrians. The snuff box had the following inscription:[123]

> This box was given as a mark of esteem and merit to Mr. North by Mr. Batty's Equestrian Company (presented by Mr. Hughes, acting manager), for the unparalleled feat of throwing 55 somersaults at one trial, at a morning performance at the Royal Leamington Spa, July 22, 1839, before Lord Dillion, Lord Manners, Countess Belgrave, Lady Paget, Marchioness of Devonshire and other ladies and gentlemen of rank and fashion.

Later, the snuff box was defaced and nearly lost in the great Chicago fire.

In the spring of 1841, North went to the West Indies for an engagement with Rufus Welch. However, on arriving in Matanzas, he found that Welch had sold his interest in the circus. His tenure with the new management developed irreconcilable differences and prompted an early mid-summer return to the mainland. He then joined "Pony" Bartlett in Baltimore, who was shortly bought out by Welch. In the fall, North went to New Orleans for an engagement with S. P. Stickney at the St. Charles Theatre. This was followed by a visit to Cuba with Sol Smith's organization. But, again, North's south-of-the-border venture proved to be unfortunate. Smith's speculation encountered competition with the Lenten season and the "red hot" *danseuse*, Fannie Ellsler, whose American tour was proving an immense success. So North went back to the comfort of Welch's welcoming arms in Baltimore.[124]

Ironically, in the spring of 1843, the two old rivals, Price and North, joined in the proprietorship of an English circus. Following the somersault-throwing contests at Astley's and North's departure from the British Isles, Price joined Ryan's company. He left it in 1841 to form his own show with William Powell, Price & Powell's Royal Circus, which toured southern England until the partnership broke up in 1843.

North went back to England in the spring of 1842. The purpose of the trip was to visit Miss Sophia West, the daughter of James West. An American trotting horse and a light buggy, which North had brought with him, were objects of curiosity to the Britishers—the horse on account of its speed and the vehicle for its frail construction. Within a short time, the long sea voyage proved fruitful. North drove his horse and buggy from Liverpool to Exeter, Devonshire, where Miss West and the American equestrian were married. Coincidentally, VanAmburgh was performing with his cats in the city at the time.[125]

In order to provide for his bride, North joined the American Company, managed by Titus, June & Sands, in Liverpool. He later appeared the London Opera House. And, then, in the spring of 1843, he combined with Price to put Price & North's Circus on the road. But, within the year, he left the circus in charge of Price and returned to the United States where he opened with Rockwell & Stone at Niblo's Garden. In the spring of 1844, he rejoined his partner in England until fall when he disposed of his interest in the show and reappeared with the American Company at the Theatre Royal, Liverpool. He was a member of Henri Franconi's Parisian company at the *Champs Élysée*, when on June 21, 1845, he appeared by royal command before King Louis of France, and the royal household, performing in the private riding school of that monarch.[126] At the end of five months he returned to the United States and was connected with the following managements: Rufus Welch, Philadelphia; Rockwell & Stone, summer 1846; John Tryon, Bowery Amphitheatre, winter 1846-47; Welch, 1847; Jones, Stickney & North, 1848; Stokes, 1849; Dan Rice, 1849-1851.

He began his own management cycle by leasing the Bowery Amphitheatre in the summer of 1851, and in the winter of 1852 conducting a circus in a riding school in Williamsburg. In 1853, North & Turner (Harry J. Turner) ran a canal boat show. In the winter season of 1853 and 1854, North leased the National Amphitheatre, Philadelphia. During the season of 1855, North & Turner traveled by wagon, and in the winter appeared in a circus which they had built in Chicago. In 1856 North erected an amphitheatre on the site of the circus. During the tenting season he turned it into a theatre where leading stars of the profession performed. Turner died during this winter, willing everything to his partner and friend. In 1857 Mr. North was elected an Alderman of Chicago, and served his term of office. In 1858-59 North's National Circus was on the road. During the summer of 1860 he ran a canal boat show and in the winter played a star engagement with Spalding & Rogers at the Bowery Theatre, New York. With a war between the states eminent in 1861, North traveled in Canada with Alexander Robinson's circus. In 1863 he associated himself with the late William Lake and Hod Norton, eventually disposing of his interests to his partners. The following year, he traveled with Haight &

DeHaven.

A New York critic wrote of his artistry astride a horse: [127]

> What Fanny Ellsler or Taglioni is to the ballet, North is to equestrian performances. It is not the mere execution of a number of difficult steps that can make a *premiere danseuse*, nor is it a number of extraordinary feats on horseback that can make the most finished rider. North, like the dancers we mention, has "caught a grace beyond the reach of art." There is a mind in almost all he does. In stature he is rather under the middle size, but well proportioned. His face is handsome and intellectual. He will be admired by everybody, but especially by the ladies. He is what Ducrow was in his prime—without exception, the most graceful and accomplished rider of the day. There are none that we have seen who can approach him.

Another scribe was quite as enthusiastic in the expression of his opinion:[128]

> There have been men of all ages of peculiar greatness, among all professions. Garrick, Betterton, Cook, Quinn, Kemble and Kean stood first in the drama. Thousands of females have equally excelled in the "fantastic toe"—but comparatively few have ever been what may be termed the "most brilliant performer in horsemanship." Mr. North stands out in bold relief of the Ring, as did Kemble of the Stage, and far excels Fanny Ellsler in his graceful motions. We doubt exceedingly whether there is a single individual can compete with Mr. North either in the beauty or in the variety of his performances

Lewis B. Lent took over the management of the Hippotheatron in November, 1865, changing the name of the arena to L. B. Lent's New York Circus. At the age of fifty-two, North made an appearance in his great specialty of the Sprite in the fairy equestrian spectacle of the "Sprites of the Silver Shower," for eight weeks, astonishing his many admirers by the evident retention of the powers of his younger days. This same year, Metcalfe & Flanagan's Olympic opened in St. Louis as a permanently located circus The performances were under the direction of North, which included a double pony act by Levi North, Jr.

Since that time he was principally in retirement. He was a man of great pride and exceptional ability in his prime, lauded by admirers on both sides of the Atlantic. It is saddening to learn that his last days were tormented by poverty and bitterness. It is said that in paying his respects to equestrian, Frank Pastor, who had died on June 25, 1885, his own demise was hastened; for in less than two weeks, on July 6, he, too, passed on.

Isaac VanAmburgh returned to the United States in 1845 and performed some ten more years with a show bearing his name. Throughout his career he had several confrontations with his animals during which he was bitten and torn. On one occasion his right wrist was severely mangled by a lion, an injury from which he never fully recovered. After retiring from the ring in the mid-1850s, he still accompanied the show in its annual tour. He died quite unexpectedly at Miller's Hotel in Philadelphia on November 29, 1865. He is remembered as a tamer of wild beast who possessed great physical strength and courage and who performed with grace, firmness, and self-possession.

Circus people have always been loyal to their own. There are many recorded incidents when performing in a town at which a former comrade is buried, the troupe would honor the memory by ceremoniously attending the grave site. In 1844, while Stickney's Circus was in Memphis, a collection was taken and a gravestone purchased and dedicated by a visit to Blackburn's resting place. The stone bore the inscription:[129]

TO THE MEMORY
OF
JOE BLACKBURN
Who Died March 26th, 1842, aged 33.
This stone was dedicated by his friends attached to
S.P. Stickney's Circus as a mark of respect,
June 3d, 1844.

Notes

PROLOGUE

[1] *New York Clipper*, February 14, 21, 28, 1880.

[2] North died in Brooklyn, N.Y., July 6, 1885, age 71.

[3] Circus buffs will recognize John Stetson as the second husband of the beautiful Katherine Stokes, equestrienne daughter of Spencer Q. Stokes.

[4] Day, "Taking One's Own Medicine"; 6.

[5] Butler, "Circus Bill Writing"; 10.

[6] E. Harper sang the number at the Richmond Hill Theatre, N.Y.C., August 31, 1836; T. D. Rice at the Bowery Theatre, N.Y.C., September 11, 1837; and J. Sanford (or Sandford) at the Franklin Theatre, N.Y.C., on October 30, 1838. [Odell, *Annals of the New York Stage*, IV; 169, 232, 306.]

[7] Durang, "The Philadelphia Stage from the Year 1794 to the Year 1855," Vol. III, Chap. 44; 259.

[8] Carter, *The Past as Prelude*; 233.

[9] *Ibid.*, 347.

[10] Thayer, *Annals*, II; 230.

[11] Day, "The Eventful Career"; 393.

[12] Thayer, II, *op. cit.*; 210.

[13] Day, "The Event Career," *op. cit.*; 393.

[14] In a communication with Day, North stated that his salary with Brown in 1835 was fourteen dollars a week. Weeks & Waring, on their way to New Orleans, offered him a bonus of $500 and a salary of twenty-five dollars a week to join them. North declined, opting to honor his contract with Brown. For this gesture of loyalty, J. Purdy raised his weekly compensation to equal the twenty-five dol-

lar offer of Weeks & Waring. [Day, "The Eventful Career," *op. cit.*, p. 393.] The circumstances here are questionable. I have found no record to confirm Weeks & Waring exhibiting in New Orleans in 1835, nor have I found any indication of a management partnership of Weeks & Waring.

[15] Durang, *op. cit.*, Vol. III, Chap. 44; 128.

[16] Ireland, *Records*, II; 123.

[17] Baker, *History of the London Stage*; 316-317, 391.

[18] Delaney, *The Story of Mobile*; 71-96.

[19] Ludlow, *Dramatic Life as I Found It*; 344.

[20] Hill did not make the crossing with Blackburn and North, but he followed shortly after.

BLACKBURN IN AMERICA

[21] Molloy, *Charleston, a Gracious Heritage*; 1-2.

[22] Durang, *op. cit.*, Chap. 42; 123.

[23] *Spirit of the Times*, June 3, 1843; 168.

[24] Ireland, II, *op. cit.*; 99.

[25] Ludlow, *op. cit.*; 327.

[26] *Spirit of the Times*, March 24, 1838; 41.

[27] Stone, "Dramatic Papers, No. II, Theatrical Reminiscences of George Stone"; 357.

[28] Blackburn or Day has made an error in indicating the date of November 22. It must be March 22.

[29] Thayer, II, *op. cit.*; 256.

[30] *Ibid.*; 255.

[31] *Spirit of the Times*, January 20, 1838, 385; February 3, 1838, 401.

[32] Ireland, II, *op. cit.*; 257.

[33] The journey to Baltimore today would be only a matter of some thirty miles.

[34] The term "squid" refers to a small firework that burned with a hissing sound.

[35] Thayer, II, *op. cit.*; 256.

[36] *Virginia, a Guide,* etc.; 170.

[37] Durang, *op. cit.*, Chap. 17, 56; Brown, *Brown's History of the American Stage*, 208.

[38] The Monday referred to was April 16. The date of Blackburn's next entry is also wrong. April 20 fell on a Friday.

[39] The play was "The Iron Chest," by George Colman, the Younger, in which evidence of murder by the villainous Mortimer, who had been acquitted of the charge, was contained in an iron chest.

[40] Thayer, II, *op. cit.*; 256.

[41] "Monsieur Tonson" was a farce by William Thomas Moncrieff. "The Kentuckian" was a revision of "The Lion of the West," a comedy by J. A. Stone.

[42] Ireland, II, *op. cit.*; 429.

[43] The reference to Monday is wrong. Monday fell on April 23. Could Tuesday have been election day?

[44] "Monsieur Mallet" was another comedy by Moncrieff; "Perfection; or, the Maid of Munster," a comedy by T. H. Bayly.

[45] Blackburn uses the expression, "shy," in assessing Cooke's stable of American trained horses. It was a favorite of his. Day explains its meaning as "queer" or "dizzy."

[46] Thayer, II, *op. cit.*; 22.

[47] *Ibid.*; 256.

[48] Wilson, *A History of the Philadelphia Stage*; 190.

[49] Thayer, II, *op. cit.*; 93.

[50] Ludlow, *op. cit.*; 326.

[51] Saxon, *Enter Foot and Horse*; 97.

[52] Durang, *op. cit.*; 150.

[53] Ireland, II, *op. cit.*; 199.

[54] Gossin did not accompany North and Blackburn to England. This may have been a barroom promise which was reconsidered in soberer moments.

[55] Thayer, II, *op. cit.*; 91, 168, 255.

[56] This would be the American Museum. The "White-haired lady" Blackburn mentions was Miss Shore, an Albino. Other attractions around this time were an ourang-outang and Signor Blitz, the magician.

[57] I can't explain the asterisks in the text, other than to assume that Day was unable to decipher Blackburn's handwriting, since he has already established a convention for omissions.

BLACKBURN IN ENGLAND

[58] Fleischer, *The Heavyweight Championship*; 36-37.

[59] Disher, *Greatest Show on Earth*, p. 192; Matlaw, ed., *American Popular Entertainment*; 199.

[60] Mitchell, *Victorian Britain*; 587-88.

[61] Ashton, *Gossip in the First Decade of Victoria's Reign*; 38.

[62] Blue Bell and Warren must have been small, stage coach depots. However, the present city of Warrington, only a short distance from Liverpool, appears to have been a logical place for a connection with the Leed's stage. "George" was a popular name for an Inn. I count at least twenty scattered about England at this time.

[63] Burke, *Travel in England*; 91-95.

[64] Eberlein and Richardson, *The English Inn, Past and Present*; 150.

[65] Besant, *Fifty Years Ago*; 33.

[66] Ashton, *When William IV Was King*; 9.

[67] FFrench, *News from the Past*; 256-57.

[68] I have no clue regarding "Conquest of Babylon." Earlier, Ducrow used a title, "The Conquest of the Amazons," which was referred to as a "cavalcade." This may have been an opening spectacle of some kind. Titles were probably invented to suit the thematic trappings of an event within the program.

[69] Hibbert, "The Circus in England"; ii.

[70] Baker, *op. cit.*; 387.

[71] Saxon, *The Life and Art of Andrew Ducrow*; 131-32.

[72] Thayer, II, *op. cit.*; 93. North once told Day about one of Sizer's principal attractions, a huge seashell, called an "oyster," which was "muscled" into the ring by several men.

[73] "Figaro," adapted from "Figaro, the Barber of Seville,"" was done as a solo scene with music by Rossini, in which Ducrow portrayed both the barber and the music teacher, Don Basilio. At this time, Ducrow was leaving the more strenuous pieces to others.

[74] "Somerstown" is, of course, a reference to Somers, N.Y., from where such a large number of showmen and performers originated.

[75] Wilson, *King Panto*; 107, 115-118.

[76] Clark was another of those circus managers who came from Astley's Amphitheatre.

[77] Wilson, *op. cit.*; 153-54.

[78] Besant, *op. cit.*; 28-29.

[79] McKechnie, *op. cit*; 51-52.

[80] Baker, *op. cit.*; 399.

[81] Lardner, *The Legendary Champions*; 26-27.

[82] This is an erroneous entry. There is no Thursday the 25th in June.

[83] Gossard, "Great Leapers," 12-13; Speaight, *A History of the Circus*, 63-65.

[84] Saxon, *op. cit.*; 154-155.

[85] Blackburn's acquaintance may have been the twenty-eight year old American actor, John Gilbert, who performed in second tragedy roles on both sides of the Atlantic.

[86] Disher, *op. cit.*; 92-93.

[87] William Bullock was a famous Drury Lane comedian who, while the theatres were closed, performed at fairs and circuses.

[88] Howard, *Prisons and Lazarettos*, Vol. I.; 243-245.

[89] Besant, *op. cit.*; 109.

[90] Hole, *English Sports and Pastimes*; 66-67.

[91] Ireland, II, *op. cit.*; 634.

[92] Saxon, *op. cit.*; 319.

[93] Ashton, *Gossip, op. cit.*; 53-59.

[94] The letter was printed in the Baltimore *Sun*. It was reprinted in the *Spirit of the Times*, August 18, 1838; 214-215.

[95] Baker, *op. cit.*; 230, 313, 416.

[96] Powell was one of the riders who attempted to copy Ducrow's style, but who fell short of equaling his model.

[97] Dick Usher was a noted pantomime clown who had worked for Ducrow in the past.

[98] Boase, III, *Modern English Biography*; 362.

[99] Turner, *Victorian Arena*; 106.

[100] *Ibid.*; 129.

[101] "The Woodcutter" may have been an arenic version of the melodrama "The Forty Thieves, or The Woodcutter of Bagdad."

[102] Ashton, *op. cit.*; 86.

[103] Phil Sampson was a major contender for the English heavyweight title but was beaten twice by Jem Ward.

[104] Fleischer, *op. cit.*; 34-36.

[105] *Bell's Life in London,* a popular Sunday weekly, first published in January 1822 by a London printer and news vendor, Robert Bell, set out to show London life "as it really was." It's original interests included police intelligence, prize fighting, horse racing, pedestrianism, and other matters about town. The paper was taken over in 1824 by William Clement, the proprietor of the *Observer*. He remained as head until his death in 1852. He brought Vincent Dowling from the *Oberver* to serve as editor, who, in his twenty-eight years at that post, made *Bell's* into a reliable and respectable sporting journal. By the year 1837 it had a weekly circulation of over 16,000. [Harris & Lee, *The Press in English Society*; 168-172; Vann & VanArsdel, *Victorian Periodicals*, 170; Jackson, *The Pictorial Press*, 224-225.]

[106] Ashton-under-Lyne is a short distance south of Hallifax, not far from Manchester.

[107] Charley Rivers was eight years old at this time.

[108] Hole, *op. cit.*; 109-113.

[109] Lardner, *op. cit.*; 9.

[110] From Manchester, the circus moved back north again to a short distance above Halifax in West Yorkshire.

[111] McKecknie, *Popular Entertainments Through the Ages*; 212-213.

[112] The jump to Sheffield took them southeast into South Yorkshire.

[113] Ireland, II, *op. cit.*; 298.

[114] Benjamin Brown, a nephew of J. Purdy Brown, managed a circus and menagerie, 1828-30, and was involved with other managers until his death in 1842.

[115] *Spirit of the Times*, November 3, 1838; 297.

[116] Saturday fell on the 15th of December.

[117] Fleischer, *op. cit.*; 47.

[118] Turner, *op. cit.*; 99.

[119] Ireland, II, *op. cit.*; 342.

EPILOGUE

[120] Turner, *op. cit.*; 11.

[121] *Ibid.*; 114.

[122] Brown, *Amphitheatres and Circuses*; 65-66. Of the men mentioned, Joseph Claveau was a clown, Fred Garson was a vaulter and clown; Herbert is unknown to me.

[123] Day, "The Eventful Career," *op. cit.*; 404.

[124] *Ibid.*

[125] North first knew VanAmburgh when he was tending bar at the Bull's Head Hotel, Philadelphia, in 1829. One of VanAmburgh's first essays in the show business was in connection with the exhibition of a hump-backed horse.

[126] Thomas Price then became the sole proprietor of Price's Circus and traveling around the continent until sometime in the 1850s when he established himself in a permanent building in Madrid with his *Circo Price*. He also had a circus in Barcelona.

[127] Day, "The Eventful Career," *op. cit.*; 81.

[128] *Ibid.*; 81-82.

[129] *Spirit of the Times*, June 29, 1844; 207.

Bibliography

BOOKS

Ashton, John. *The Dawn of the XIXth Century in England*. London: T. Fisher Unwin, 1906.

——————. *Gossip in the First Decade of Victoria's Reign*. London: Hurst & Blackett, Ltd., 1903.

——————. *When William IV Was King*. London: Chapman & Hall, Ltd., 1896.

Baker, H. Barton. *History of the London Stage*. New York: Benjamin Blom (reissue), 1969.

Besant, Walter. *Fifty Years Ago*. New York: Harper & Brothers, 1888.

Boase, Frederick. *Modern English Biography*, Vols. I-VI. London: Truro, Netherton & Worth, 1892-1921.

Brown, T. Allston (edited by William L. Slout). *Amphitheatres and Circuses*. San Bernardino (CA): The Borgo Press, 1994.

——————. *History of the American Stage*. New York: Benjamin Blom (reissue), 1969.

——————. *History of the New York Stage*, 3 vols. New York: Benjamin Blom (reissue), 1964.

Burke, Thomas. *The Streets of London*. London: B. T. Batsford, Ltd, 1940.

——————. *Travel in England*. London: B.T. Bratsford Ltd., 1942.

Carter, Hodding, editor-in-chief, *The Past as Prelude*. New Orleans: Pelican Publishing House, 1968.

Chindahl, George L. *A History of the Circus in America*. Caldwell, Idaho: Caxton Printers, 1959.

Clapp, William A. *A Record of the Boston Stage*. New York: Greenwood Press (reissue), 1969.

Day, Charles H. (edited by William L. Slout). *Ink from a Circus Press Agent*. San Bernardino (CA): The Borgo Press, 1995.

Delaney, Caldwell. *The Story of Mobile*. Mobile: Gill Press, (reissue), 1962.

Disher, M. Willson. *Greatest Show on Earth*. New York: Benjamin Blom (reissue), 1971.

Durang, Charles (edited by William L. Slout), *The Theatrical Rambles of Mr. and Mrs. John Greene*. San Bernardino (CA): The Borgo Press, 1987.

Eberlein, Harold Donaldson and A.E. Richardson. *The English Inn, Past and Present*. Philadelphia: J.B. Lippincott Co., 1926.

Fleischer, Nat. *The Heavyweight Championship*. New York: G.P. Putnam's Sons, 1949.

FFrench, Yvonne. *News from the Past, the Autobiography of the 19th Century*. New York: Viking Press.

Frost, Thomas. *Circus Life and Circus Celebrities*. London: Tinsley Brothers, 1875.

Gorn, Elliott J. *The Manly Art*. Ithaca: Cornell University Press, 1986.

Grombach, John V. *The Saga of the Fist*. New York: A.S. Barnes and Company, 1949.

Harris, Michael and Alan Lee, eds. *The Press in English Society from the Seventeenth to Nineteenth Centuries*. London: Associated University Presses, 1986.

Hole, Christina. *English Sports and Pastimes*. London: B.T. Batsford Ltd., 1949.

Howard, John. *Prisons and Lazarettos*, Vol. I. Montclair, NJ.: Patterson Smith (reissue), 1973.

Ireland, Joseph N. *Records of the New York Stage from 1750 to 1860*, 2 vols. New York: T. H. Morrell, 1867.

Jackson, Mason. *The Pictorial Press*. London: Hurst & Blackett, 1885.

James, Reese D. *Old Drury of Philadelphia, A History of the Philadelphia Stage, 1800-1835*. Philadelphia: University of Pennsylvania Press, 1935.

Kendall, John S. *The Golden Age of the New Orleans Theatre*. Baton Rouge: Louisiana State University Press, 1952.

Lardner, Rex. *The Legendary Champions*. New York: American Heritage Press, 1972.

Ludlow, Noah M. *Dramatic Life as I Found It*. New York: Benjamin Blom (reissue), 1966.

Matlaw, Myron, ed. *American Popular Entertainment*: George Speaight, "The Origin of the Circus Parade Wagon." Westwood, CT: Greenwood Press, 1977.

McKechnie, Samuel. *Popular Entertainments Through the Ages*. New York: Benjamin Blom (reissue), 1969.

Molloy, Robert, *Charleston, a Gracious Heritage*. New York: D. Appleton-Century company, Inc., 1947.

Mordecal, Samuel. *Virginia, Especially Richmond, in By-Gone Days*. Richmond: West & Johnston, Publishers, 1860.

Odell, George C. D. *Annals of the New York Stage*, Vols. I-VIII. New York: Columbia University Press, 1927-31.

Saxon, A.H. *Enter Foot and Horse*. New Haven: Yale University Press, 1968.

_____. *The Life and Art of Andrew Ducrow*. Archon Books, 1978.

Slout, William L. *A Biographical Dictionary of the 19th Century American Circus* (unpublished manuscript), 1992.

Smither, Nelle Kroger. *A History of the English Theatre in New Orleans.* New York: Benjamin Blom (reissue), 1967.

South Carolina, compiled by workers of the Writers' Program of the Works Progress Administration, South Carolina. New York: Oxford University Press, 1941.

Speaight, George. *A History of the Circus.* London: The Tantivy Press, 1980.

Thayer, Stuart. *Annals of the American Circus, 1793-1829*, Vol. I, Manchester, MI, 1976.

_____. *Annals of the American Circus, 1830-1847*, Vol. II Seattle: Peanut Butter Publishing, Inc., 1986.

Turner, John. *Victorian Arena: The Performers.* Liverpool:Lingdales Press, 1995.

Vann, J. Don and Rosemary T. VanArsdel, eds. *Victorian Periodicals.* New York: The Modern Language Association of America, 1978.

Virginia, a Guide to the Old Dominion. Compiled by workers of the Writers' Program of the W.P.A. New York: Oxford University Press, 1940.

Walton, John K. and James Walvin, eds. *Leisure in Britain, 1780-1939.* Manchester: Manchester University Press, 1983.

Wilson, A.E. *King Panto.* New York: E.P. Dutton & Co., Inc., 1935.

Wilson, Arthur Herman. *A History of the Philadelphia Theatre, 1835-55.* Philadelphia: University of Pennsylvania Press, 1935.

ARTICLES
Bowen, Albert R., "The Circus in Rural Missouri," *Missouri Historical Review*, October, 1952.

"Brief Reminiscences of the Circus in Days of Yore: The Old Richmond Hill," *New York Clipper*, October 8, 1864.

"Broadway Circus," *New York Clipper*, November 30, 1878.

Butler, Roland, "Circus Bill Writing and Men Who Made It an Art," *Billboard*, March 22, 1924.

Day, Charles H., "A Clown's Log, Extracts from the Diary of the Late Joseph Blackburn, Chronicling Incidents of Travel with Circuses in the United States and England Forty Years Ago, with His Opinions of and Allusions to Professionals of the Period," *New York Clipper*, February 14, 21, 28, 1880.

_____, "The Eventful Career of Levi J. North," *New York Clipper*, March 6, 13, 1880.

_____, "Taking One's Own Medicine," *Billboard*, April 6, 1901, p. 6.

Durang, Charles, "The Philadelphia Stage from the Year of 1794 to the Year 1855," Philadelphia *Weekly Dispatch*, 1854-60. (Microfilm) in three parts, beginning with issue of May 7, 1854.

"Echoes of a Famous Ring: The Gala Days of the Old Bowery Amphitheatre," *New York Clipper*, April 8, 1876.

Gossard, Steve, "Frank Gardner and the Great Leapers," *Bandwagon*, July-August 1990.

Hibbert, Henry George, "The Circus in England," *New York Clipper*, February 19, 1910.

Stone, George, *New York Clipper*, "Dramatic Papers No. II," February 23, 1861.

PERIODICALS

Bell's Life in London and Sporting Chronicle (microfilm}, 1837-38.

New York Clipper, Vols. 1-62, May 7, 1853 through July 12, 1924.

Spirit of the Times, Vols. 1-30, December 10, 1831 through February 2, 1861.

INDEX

Printed in July 2019
by Rotomail Italia S.p.A., Vignate (MI) - Italy